Better Homes and Gardens®

HOME LANDSCAPING

Plants, Projects, and Ideas for Your Yard

Better Homes and Gardens® Books
Des Moines

BETTER HOMES AND GARDENS® BOOKS
An Imprint of Meredith® Books

HOME LANDSCAPING
Writers
 Landscaping: Jeff Cox
 Projects: David W. Toht, Steve Cory
Associate Art Director: Tom Wegner
Designer: Michael Burns
Project Plans: Dave Toht, Steve Cory
Copy Editors: Ron Harris, Kay Sanders,
 Mary Helen Schiltz
Indexer: Kathleen Poole
Production Manager: Douglas Johnston

Director, New Product Development:
 Ray Wolf
Managing Editor: Christopher Cavanaugh

Meredith Publishing Group
President, Publishing Group:
 Christopher Little
Vice President and Publishing Director:
 John P. Loughlin

Meredith Corporation
Chairman of the Board and Chief Executive
 Officer: Jack D. Rehm
President and Chief Operating Officer:
 William T. Kerr

Chairman of the Executive Committee:
 E. T. Meredith III

Photographers:

Alan Abramowitz: 75
Thomas Arledge: 82
Ernie Braun: 17 (top right), 28, 113
Kim Brun: 88, 99
David Cavagnaro: 14, 16, 19, 29 (left), 39, 44, 54, 59, 72, 76 (top right), 79, 83 (top left), 94, 110, 116, 132–133, 141, 174, 182, 184, 184–185, 194, 198
Stephen Cridland: 22 (top left), 51, 65 (top right), 102
R. Todd Davis: 143, 170, 170–171, 177, 178, 179 (top right), 183
Randy Foulds: 11 (bottom), 34
George deGennaro: 57, 63
Susan Gilmore: 42
Ed Gohlich: 6–7, 22 (bottom right), 23, 43 (top right), 114
Karlis Grants: 15 (bottom), 30–31, 41, 104–105, 131, 172
Bob Hawks: 13
Bill Helms: 146
Saxon Holt: 15 (top), 20, 24, 35 (bottom right), 45 (bottom left), 46, 46–47, 52, 55, 56 (right), 69, 109, 112, 122, 123, 126, 132, 140, 181, back cover (top left and top right)
Jon Jensen: 17 (bottom left)
Gene Johnson: 12, 48 (right), 53 (left), 67 (top left), back cover (center)
Dency Kane: 137, 176, 180
Peter Krumhardt: 95, 134, 138, 148, 161
Barbara Martin: 96, 135, 144
Maris/Semel: 38, 61, 89, 91, 111, 136, 154
D. McConnell: front cover and 200-201
Jerry Pavia: 8, 10, 11 (top), 18, 21, 25, 26 (bottom left), 27, 30, 32, 33, 36, 37, 40, 43 (bottom left), 45 (top right), 48 (left), 49, 50 (right), 56 (left), 64, 65 (bottom left), 66, 68, 69 (bottom right), 72–74, 76, 78, 80, 81, 83 (bottom right), 84, 85, 100, 101, 106–108, 115, 118–121, 124, 125, 127, 128, 169, 179 (bottom left), 196, 197, back cover (bottom left)
PHOTO NATS: 60, 62, 142, 153, 155, 156, 159, 164, 165, 173, 186–190, 192, 193, 195
Mary Carolyn Pindar: 67 (bottom right), 92, 97
Susan Roth: 93, 150, 150–151, 158, 160, 166, 175
Linda Smith: 104, 139
Bill Stites: 86–87, 90, 152, 168
Rick Taylor: 8–9, 26 (top right), 50 (left), 58, 117
Philip Thompson: 18 (bottom right)
Joan Vanderschmitt: 35 (top left), 53 (right)
Jessie Walker: 86
Judy Watts: 103 and back cover (bottom right)

A home garden and landscape
should reflect your personal interests and sense of
beauty. This book is designed to give you simple,
basic approaches to planting your property for visual
appeal and practicality. Our hope is that you will imbue
these techniques and approaches with your own
ideas about what is beautiful.

Where do you start? Literary and artistic references can
help spark new ideas for your garden. By far the
most important source of landscaping ideas, however, is
your memories of gardens and natural places—a special
spot from your childhood, such as a path through shrubbery and over long meadow grasses that leads to a hidden swimming hole, a garden behind your grandmother's
house where colorful dahlias grew, or aromatic bunches
of wild grapes you discovered on vines
laced through roadside hedgerows.

By following the ideas and suggestions in this book, you
can beautify your property, add to its value, and bring
it to life by injecting your personality and style into the
mix. After all, the best gardens embody something
of their makers. The more meaning you put into your
landscaping, the more you will enjoy it and
treasure it over the years.

CONTENTS

CONTENTS

PART ONE:
THE LANDSCAPE

THE FRONT YARD

THE FRONT YARD

Ornamental plants in a pink and silver theme smother a bermed slope, softening the stark front of this modern house and offering privacy as well as beauty.

Landscaping Tip:
Create a fence or barrier between the front of your property and the street or neighboring property.

Putting a pretty face on your property by landscaping your front yard makes good sense. The front yard is the face your house turns to the world, and everyone likes to make a good impression.

A beautiful front yard welcomes you home with style, reflecting your sense of beauty and satisfying your need for harmony. It provides spaces to showcase features like flower beds and borders, a beautiful wall, an interesting flagstone walkway, and even pools and water plants. And it adds value to your property should it come time to sell. Real estate agents estimate handsome landscaping can boost the value of a property by as much as a third.

The typical front yard contains considerable unused and wasted space. Often a high-maintenance turf lawn starts at the street and runs to the front of a house that rises from a border of evergreen shrubbery. If you want to use the lawn as a place to relax and read the paper, play badminton, or practice chipping

golf balls, you do it in full view of everyone in the neighborhood. The front yard often provides little privacy, interest, and value. Instead, it is a place of work: a vast expanse that needs to be mowed and trimmed again and again throughout the summer.

On the following pages, we'll suggest ways you can gain some privacy, show you how to add interest to your yard, and assess your front yard's value as a place you and your family can use and enjoy.

FENCES AND WALLS

Nothing enhances privacy more than a fence with a gated entrance. One of the prettiest entrances can be created by training 'New Dawn'—a well-behaved, semidouble rambling rose of softest blush pink—over a trellised archway above a garden gate.

Not every home and front yard should be fenced, but it's an option to consider. Fencing a front yard provides security, keeps pets and children from roaming the neighborhood, supports climbing and flowering plants such as roses and clematis, and provides a backdrop for beds of perennial and annual flowering plants around its perimeter.

A fence in the front yard (left) offers security and adds an architectural element to a riotous profusion of flowering plants.

An old-fashioned pink rose climbs a fence, then an arbor (above), to reach the white hydrangea on the other side. The eye-catching entry welcomes the visitor and shields the front porch from full view.

A low, rustic fence complements a ranch-style house with its strong horizontal lines. The fence, more decorative than practical, is underplanted with assorted flowers.

In the United States, the white picket fence is typical; both pretty and friendly, it provides some security and supports a wide variety of flowering plants. Less typical is the black wrought-iron fence, which can support flowering vines and roses and provide security but generally appears less friendly than a picket fence.

Tall, solid fencing of closely spaced boards tells the world that you prize privacy and creates a secure barrier against intruders. Planting choices for solid fencing are limited to climbers that reach the top and tumble over, such as wisteria, ivy, pyracantha, or climbing roses.

Instead of a fence, consider a brick or stone wall. Although less popular than fences,

This house with multipaned windows suggests New England. In the yard, the colonial look of red brick and white picket fencing beautifully complements its style.

brick walls are secure and provide wonderful support and background for flowering plants because of their dull, earthy colors. Low stone walls are less secure than brick, but they can be beautiful barriers for bordering a street. The natural look of stone enhances all manner of plants.

Dense, impenetrable shrubbery or hedges—especially thorny or prickly roses, hollies, firethorn, or the like—can perform the same function as a fence or wall. If the shrubs are dark evergreens, such as yews, they form a dark, dramatic backdrop for flower gardens with jeweled colors.

ROLE OF FENCING

On the street or entrance side, you can edge a fence with flowers, which connotes a welcome from the folks within, or you can let it stand unadorned as a gentle rebuff to those who would impinge on your privacy.

From inside, a fence stops the eye, so the landscape doesn't simply run into the street. It allows you to create a garden with boundaries, which provides a precise space to comprehend.

Fencing also lends an architectural element to the front landscape. Consider, for example, the yard with no architecture, containing only shrubbery, trees, flowering plants, and lawn that begins at the front door and melts away into the distance. Green and leafy, with perhaps color from flowers, such a yard creates the same sense of unrelieved vegetation that you encounter in a wood or meadow.

Now imagine the front yard with a lawn and fence but no plantings. The landscaping suggests confinement and stark discipline.

The crisscross lath work of this unusual fence echoes the design of the porch enclosure. The swayed top rail gives a soft curve to the angular house front. A planting of flowers artfully hides the bottom of the fence.

13

Forsythia planted behind this picket fence erupts in an explosion of gold in early spring. The combination of fence and dense forsythia is not only beautiful but also securely separates the front yard from the street.

walkway. Use plants that increase in height as you move toward the fence—just as you would arrange people of different heights for a photograph so that everyone can be seen.

Place a few taller plants spotted here and there at the low, front edge of the border so they spill out onto the lawn or path. They interrupt the regularity of having all low plants in front and add visual excitement. An ornamental grass or a long-leaved crocosmia is a good choice for an interrupter; the slender leaves arch out and down to the ground. Daylilies also are effective.

Finally, contemplate a yard with lawn and plants well mixed with the architectural element of the fence. Here the curves of the greenery both contrast and complement the straight lines of the fence. This principle of contrast and complement is central to all landscaping design.

CHOOSING PLANTS

Above all, fencing creates a backdrop for a border of flowering plants. When you plant a garden that borders a fence, start with small, low-growing plants at the lawn's edge or

If your fence is wood, site plants so the border doesn't quite reach the fence. This gives you room to work between the fence and the plants to maintain the plantings in summer. The tall plants in the back will spread out and engulf the fence, but judicious shearing or pruning a couple of times a year will keep the path open between fence and border. If you live in an area with lots of summer rainfall, you may find snails and slugs where wet vegetation is crammed onto the fence. Prevent the problem by keeping the fence relatively free and open to the drying air.

The fence (left) couldn't be simpler, but the plant selection is carefully chosen to mix foliage color with flower color. The garden builds from street level to a sheltering height behind the fence.

The blue-and-white color scheme of the house (right) is repeated in the front garden. Blue and white delphiniums and other flowers are accented with strong, pure reds. Notice how the plantings shield the front door of the house.

Given a straight walkway to work with, a clever gardener suggests a sinuous path by edging it with curving drifts of Coreopsis verticillata, Echinacea purpurea, *grasses, lilies, and phlox.*

Whether you choose fence, wall, or hedge, allow for air flow by using airy shrubs, spaces between boards, or latticework to provide gaps in the barrier. Too much barrier interrupts cooling westerly air flow in the afternoon. If the barrier is placed at the bottom of a slope, it will be frost-prone because cold air sinks and stays there.

If you have a corner lot, you actually have two front yards, which doubles your need for privacy. Extend the fence or hedging on two sides of the property, or fence the frontage along one street and plant hedging along the other to differentiate between the two areas.

PATHS AND WALKWAYS

Add interest to a formal approach to the front door by making the walkway meander. If the path is straight and made of something moveable, such as bricks or fieldstone, reshape it so that it curves.

Create several kinds of planting beds alongside the walkway: a small perennial border, an island bed of mixed woody and herbaceous plants, different-colored evergreen shrubs in a round bed tucked into a curve of the walkway, and a raised wall or rock garden berm planted with miniatures and Alpine plants. Incorporate some surprises: a patch of ever-blooming 'Stella de Oro' daylilies (*Hemerocallis*), a bushy specimen of 'Pink Breath of Heaven' (*Coleonema*) to pinch and smell, or a planting of fine Alpine strawberries (*Fragaria vesca*). Give some thought to what you'd like to discover on this miniature journey to your front door and provide it.

CREATING AN ILLUSION

You also can add interest by pretending that the walkway is something else—a riverbed, for example, with the banks of the river being

the areas to the right and left. You might plant a long drift of ornamental grass, such as the grasses that border a meandering meadow stream. Add a weeping Higan cherry reminiscent of willows that trail their green fingers in the water.

Pretending gives you an idea to work with, so you can transform your landscape from ordinary to extraordinary.

You also might pretend the walkway is the entrance path to the Garden of Eden, where fruit grew for the asking. Plant beds with sweet things to eat:

A curving walkway to the front door lessens the strict formality of the house front. Notice how the gardener echoed the house colors with her choice of flowering plants.

gooseberries, raspberries of all types, red and black currants, grapes, and lots of dwarf apples, peaches, plums, cherries, and apricots. What a wonderful message to send to visitors!

You could build a walkway that dissolves into paths that lead to a series of raised beds planted with your favorite ornamentals or vegetables. Who says you can't grow squash in the front yard?

This walk meanders in a gentle curve to the front door, creating a delightful transition between the flower border and the lawn.

Landscaping Tip:
Create screens that separate the yard into discrete areas and hide the front door from the most frequently used approach.

SLOPE SOLUTIONS

Some houses are built atop slopes that descend to street level. Homeowners often consider slopes to be problem areas, but they actually offer wonderful opportunities for creative landscaping.

Instead of a flat walkway, sloping yards have steps and may have landings from the street to the house. Think of the steps and landings as viewing platforms. The sloping ground on both sides provides gallery space

Instead of a formal, high-maintenance front lawn, this turn-of-the-century house features an informal—and low-maintenance—naturalistic planting of yellow daylilies, gold rudbeckia, reddish sedum 'Autumn Joy,' ornamental grasses, and birches.

A wooden retaining wall and terraces allow for mixed plantings that soften the stark lines of this house built atop a small slope.

for presenting plants. Here you can show-case beautiful flower beds, specimen trees, favorite groupings of shrubs, or natural-istic combinations of rocks and plants.

Terracing slopes allows you to spot-light plants that tumble over walls, giving a hanging-gardens effect, and helps solve hillside erosion problems.

SCREENING FOR PRIVACY

Although you need a path from the street to the front door, you don't have to see the door. Create landscaping that hides the front door so that traversing the walkway is an intriguing adventure.

This is possible even with a small front yard if a screen is built or planted between the entrance to the yard and the door. (Tall woven fences, high hedges, or a group of dense evergreens all make good screens.) A screen should simply block the view to the front door from the direction of most frequent approach.

It's fine if the front door is seen from other angles. In fact, you may want neighbors to be able to see your front door for security reasons. (Also consider installing security lighting in your front yard—lights that illuminate the front steps and doorway, the driveway entrance, and any areas of dark shrubbery.)

You can use screening in other parts of the front yard as well. Usually, you drive into your property, rather than enter through a formal front gate and walkway, so go to the driveway or garage and look toward the house. If you can see the front door, think about how you might screen it from view.

Two magnificent golden Chamae-cyparis *flank an entrance, screening most of the house and front gate from the street. Other large evergreens, such as junipers, yews, cypresses, and spruces, would perform a similar function in varied shades of green, gold, or blue.*

A collection of color-coordinated pots and interesting plantings not only screens the front of the house but also draws the eye away from the building into the garden in the foreground.

Yards of any size should be planted so that some areas are visually shielded from others. A yard where everything can be seen from any vantage point offers little mystery or visual allure.

Screens shouldn't chop the front yard in two, and they shouldn't interrupt the architectural lines of the house. Screens or trees that create discrete zones should be placed to frame the house. They should flank the sides and soften the edges rather than jut up awkwardly in the middle of the building.

Screens can change with the seasons. A flowering crab apple or doublefile viburnum underplanted with tall perennials serves as a screen in the summer but leaves the house visible through the delicate structure of the tree in winter.

A screened front door provides privacy, but not every front door needs it. Sometimes it is best to make the door the focal point of a landscape design. The door becomes a focal

This flowering fantasy of a front yard is for the family only, as little of it can be seen from the street. It's the kind of landscape that a small child will remember throughout life, and someday try to emulate with a garden of his or her own.

Favored plants of the Victorian era are the perfect choice to landscape this magnificent old Victorian frame house (left) with its classic picket fence.

Landscaping Tip:

Tie the house to the landscape by using plantings that hide parts of the building and harmonize with the shape of the house.

Plantings that mount to a high point in the center of the flower bed partially hide the entrance and tie the house (right) to its yard.

point when the walkway leading to it is flanked by dramatic beds of carefully chosen plants. Such a formal approach is achieved with symmetry, by planting both sides of the walkway with the same plants in the same pattern.

TIES THAT BIND

Whatever the setting, front-yard landscaping should tie the house to the site. Beds, borders, shrubbery, and trees strategically placed along the foundation soften the transition from the horizontal ground level to the vertical house walls. Using foundation plants to repeat the shape of a feature of the house is an effective technique. For example, echo front-porch pillars with vertical junipers or the shape of a large decorative urn turned upside down to resemble a clipped yew.

Similar materials and finishes also tie the house to the land. If the house is painted white, an arbor or patio edge that protrudes from the house into the landscape might also be painted white. A brick house can be tied to its site by a series of brick walks or a patio leading to the house. A house atop a slope needs the terraced straight lines of decking or

patios descending by levels to make it look like part of the land instead of a box perched on top of a round ball.

ADDING INTEREST

The ways the front yard can be made more interesting are limited only by your imagination. For instance, the walkway might begin as concrete but have bricks sparsely

The color and pattern of the bricks in this front entrance and walkway echo the architecture and color of the house, tying the building to its site.

Although useful, lawn grasses are not very interesting. Here pools of contrasting purple ajuga and green ground covers replace grass, creating an eye-catching approach to the house.

the deciduous 'Galaxy' magnolia, and the disease-resistant Chinese elm (*Ulmus parvifolia*) variety called 'Dynasty.'

GIVE THE YARD A FACE-LIFT

If you own an old property that was planted years ago, you may face overgrown foundation plantings that have grown together, blocking the view from the windows and putting the house into perpetual shadow. Be ruthless when revitalizing an old property and let some sunshine in.

First, visualize the house with all the old foundation plants removed. Next visualize or sketch the landscaping of your dreams. If existing shrubs or trees fit this idea, save them. If they need cutting back or thinning, do it vigorously. If they don't fit your new plans, remove them. Think twice, however, before removing any beautiful or rare old specimens. Consider asking a professional to look at your plantings and assess their worth if you're uncertain about their value.

LOW-MAINTENANCE OPTIONS

Be sure to include some lawn in your landscape for strolling or lolling, but not so much that weekends in summer mean

inset after 10 feet or so. As you traverse the walkway, more bricks replace the concrete until only bricks are used. But then, here and there, small cobbles appear interspersed among the bricks, until, after some yards, the bricks are gone and the walkway is made entirely of cobbles. Such a progression through different interesting materials and varying patterns within those materials could continue to the front door.

If you've bought a new house, you can add interest to the front yard by choosing trees that are more exciting and less problem-prone than traditional favorites like Norway maples, tulip poplars, and white birches. Instead, choose superior trees like the rich coral-pink-flowered 'Tuscarora' crape myrtle,

walking miles behind a lawn mower. Instead of an expansive lawn, keep it simple and small, and replace most of the grass with ground covers, herbs for the kitchen or bath, or other low-maintenance plants.

Ground covers mixed with shrubs and small understory trees cut the heavy maintenance that lawns require and keep people within bounds. Visitors and family members are unlikely to trample beds of rock cotoneaster or periwinkle. If they do, install a path, because the trampling is being done to get somewhere. In fact, make sure you notice traffic flows of adults, children, and dogs before you install low-maintenance ground covers. Build paths to help people get where they want to go.

To convert lawn to ground covers, start in the spring. Remove the sod in 2-foot-wide strips and stack them upside down. This hastens rotting. After the strips have decomposed, return the topsoil to bare spots or place it around trees and shrubs. An alternative to removing sod is to smother it with black plastic. Use clear plastic in sunny locations because the heat buildup will soon kill the grass.

Once the grass is killed or removed, improve the soil with compost and plant ground covers, spacing as your nursery recommends. For example, hostas and sedum should be planted 12 to 18 inches apart; ajuga, 6 to 8 inches apart; and creeping phlox, 6 to 12 inches apart.

Mulch around your new plants to suppress weeds. Use a mulch that decays rapidly, such as grass clippings or other finely shredded

A red flowering quince (Chaenomeles spp.) and a border of soft, gray-green herbs and perennials set off an undulating carpet of low-growing thyme.

Landscaping Tip:

Reduce the amount of grass and increase plantings of low-maintenance ground covers, flower beds, and patches of shrubbery.

Mixed hues of African daisies interspersed with islands of dark green manzanita (below) bring a torrent of color to what was once a dull green lawn.

This planting of pachysandra colonizing an area of deep mulch (right) is the perfect low-maintenance lawn alternative. It takes little care other than pulling the odd weed. Rain usually supplies all the water it needs.

Foundation plantings once were limited to a handful of evergreen shrubs, but no longer. Here gray-green lamb's ears (Stachys byzantina) and spiky lavenders, along with the pink and yellow flowers in the background, make strong color harmony with the house.

plant material mixed with a little nitrogenous material, such as aged manure. The plants will grow into the mulched spaces and become a mat that weeds cannot penetrate.

GROUND-COVER OPTIONS

You can mix and match ground covers in almost any color of the rainbow, texture, and shape, and for any conditions in your garden. Ground covers come in an array of colors:

- black—black mondo grass (*Ophiopogon planiscapus* 'Nigrescens')
- dark green—ajuga (*Ajuga*)
- medium green—pachysandra (*Pachysandra*)
- light green or yellow—Scotch moss (*Sagina subulata* 'Aurea')
- lavender-mauve—*Echeveria* 'Afterglow'
- red—certain dwarf barberries
- silver—*Lamium maculatum* 'Beacon Silver' and many artemisias
- coral—*Phormium tenax* 'Maori Sunrise'
- beige—many ornamental grasses after frost
- white—dusty miller (*Senecio cineraria*)
- variegated—*Houttuynia cordata, Euonymus fortunei*, variegated ivies, and many hostas

The use of ground covers to replace lawn is one of the cutting-edge movements in modern landscaping, and an exciting area in which to work. You'll find more information on using ground covers in later chapters.

Chubby piceas and low junipers mix with rocks and colorful flowers in this artful approach to the front door. Landscaping is at its best when it shows off the aesthetic sense of the gardener.

FRONT AND CENTER

The front yard is for showcasing and for greeting the world. Here you can display your horticultural gems, such as a tamarisk (*Tamarix*) that covers itself with soft, dusty, rose-pink fluff in spring, or a fine specimen of dramatic oak-leaf hydrangea (*Hydrangea quercifolia*).

It's also where you should incorporate your most exciting landscaping ideas. For example, combine a small tree with pink flower candles called pink summersweet (*Clethra alnifolia* 'Rosea') with big blue lilyturf (*Liriope muscari*) planted beneath it. Both the summersweet and the lilyturf bloom in high summer. The combination is spectacular, featuring pink flowers above and deep blue-purple flowers below. The summersweet develops extraordinarily bright fall color. The lilyturf has tidy, grasslike leaves that are attractive throughout the year.

The front yard is also a place for more mundane doings. The dog may spend time in a fenced portion of the yard, providing protection and an early warning system if someone arrives unannounced. Or you may wash the car there; if you do, plant something tough and soil-hugging, such as *Phlox subulata*, to prevent erosion. You also may want to prevent the neighborhood dogs and kids from traipsing through your yard; a thick barrier of blackberries can accomplish this. The dogs turn aside, and the kids stop to sample the blackberries.

ROOMS WITH A VIEW

As you landscape your front yard, don't forget to consider the views from inside the house. Don't block the view from a well-frequented

These pink and red roses add beauty to the window from the outside and frame the view from the inside with sweet colors.

window by planting a screen there. Develop gardens that will be attractive from windows, especially in winter, when you spend more time indoors. Be especially careful when developing gardens viewed from the kitchen, a living room picture window, and indoor/outdoor spaces such as patios, decks, and porches, where people spend a lot of leisure time.

Because many houses are oriented with the front to the south, the front yard is an ideal site for an attached sunroom or solar greenhouse. Such an addition allows you to continue growing flowering plants through the winter or start seedlings in the spring. A sunroom also provides free solar heat if you

install large doors that open to the interior. It will be your favorite place for coffee on sunny winter mornings.

In pleasant weather, you can open these sunspaces to the outside. Plant deciduous trees to shade the sunroom in summer. If your area is buggy, create screening so the sunspace can be a shady, screened-in porch in summer.

Pruning the lower branches of this magnificent tree allows the owners of the house to enjoy the view from their downstairs windows. The tree still provides privacy and adds inestimable beauty to the front yard.

29

THE SIDE YARD

Both sides of this path to the back yard are planted as a mixed border, with strong vertical evergreens and horizontal red roses. The climbing white rose beautifully softens the corner of the porch. This path invites exploration.

Landscaping Tip:

Slow the pace of those using the side yard by narrowing the walkway and making steps and corners a part of it.

Landscaping your side yard adds interesting and usable space to your property. Because it is often a long, narrow area or lacks a well-defined purpose, homeowners tend to ignore the side yard and use it only to funnel people between the front and back yards.

The side yard may have a path or perfunctory flower beds or shrubs along a fence to dress it up, but it frequently lacks a planned landscape with real character. This is a waste, because the side yard can be a spot for quiet relaxation, discovery, or the display of choice plants, singly or as a marriage of perfect partners.

Most houses have two side yards, so you can accommodate the practical as well as the ornamental. One yard can be used as a thoroughfare, and the other can be designed and landscaped for a more leisurely purpose. The latter is the focus of this chapter.

If you have a narrow side yard, you're fortunate, because it gives you limits within which to work. As any artist will tell you, a limited palette produces more cohesive results than one from which anything is possible.

DOWN THE GARDEN PATH

To slow traffic between the front and back yards, channel visitors into a path made for strolling and encourage them to stay on it. The more a path requires visitors to keep their eyes on their footing, the slower they will go. Narrow the path. Interrupt it with stepping-stones interplanted with low-growing ground covers bordered by higher vegetation. Steps and corners also will slow visitors.

Turning corners means that the view through the side yard is obstructed by one or more barriers, which stop the line of sight and force visitors to turn. If the landscaping is cleverly done, visitors will encounter unexpected beauty along the way.

Your side yard may be bounded on one side by a house or garage wall and on the other by a fence, trees and shrubs, flower borders, or open land. If there is no barrier at the edge of your property and the side

yard adjoins open land or a neighboring yard, consider installing a tall fence or hedging near the house. This contributes privacy, a dramatic backdrop for plants, and shade for a west wall if the house faces south.

A fence also turns the side yard into a canyon flanked by a house wall and the tall fence or hedge. This passage can include stepping-stones; twists and turns around barriers or obstacles; steps up and down; and interesting and beautiful plantings, architecture, and ornamentation.

From the interesting pattern of the paving stones to the burnished gold rose and coordinated colors of the other plants, this side yard establishes a strong, cohesive visual statement. The plain backdrop of the fence helps define the elements.

The gardener filled this side yard with perennial borders that look good from the path and give a pleasing view from the bay windows that overlook the garden.

POINTS OF VIEW

How do you create such a space? Begin with windows that face the side yard, especially large or featured windows, such as a bay. Look out those windows. Is the view interesting? If there is no fence and the view includes a nice, long vista that you wish to keep, consider incorporating 7-foot-high hedging or fencing up to that spot, lowering the barrier to about 3 feet so that the long view is maintained from the window, and raising it back up to its full 7 feet beyond the window.

Another option is to build a section of wall with a moon gate directly across from the window. Moon gates are large, round holes, often seen in Chinese garden walls. Vistas beyond are glimpsed partially, intriguing viewers by a suggestion of another world.

If you don't have a long vista worth keeping and you plan to build a solid fence along the edge of the property to create a narrow canyon, use the area across from the windows for exquisite flower borders, mixed borders with shrubs, or spectacular specimen plants. To enhance the attractiveness of many specimen shrubs and small trees, prune lower limbs to reveal the plant's woody structure. Further yearly pruning will shape that woody structure into living sculpture.

ELEMENTS OF STYLE

An arbor, especially one that attaches to the house on one side and extends to the fence or hedging on the other side, is a wonderful element for the side yard. Plant it with grapes, such as the delicious, seedless Einset variety; climbing roses, such as 'Climbing Iceberg' or 'Don Juan'; one of the incredibly beautiful varieties of clematis; or fragrant wisteria paired with yellow 'Lady Banks' roses. Your choices of plants for the arbor are many. The effect is always magical as the

Imagine this narrow side yard (left) without the arbor. It would be much less interesting. The arbor confines the path, then releases it into the larger sitting area. The confine-and-release technique adds drama and mystery to a garden.

path takes you under the arbor's waterfall of fruit and flowers.

To make your long, narrow side yard appear shorter and more compact, place large-leaved plants in the center and smaller-leaved ones at each end. Whichever way you enter the yard, large-leaved plants will be

Restrained color in the cool side yard (right) and the partial view of an intriguing, sunny back yard beyond the arbor encourage visitors to traverse the path to see what lies beyond.

35

An exquisite choice of plants turns this narrow side yard border and fence into a tableau suggesting greater depth. Hostas, a five-fingered fern, Solomon's-seal, and Clematis montana on the fence are an inspired grouping.

toward you and smaller-leaved ones will be behind them. To lengthen the yard, place smaller-leaved plants toward you and larger-leaved plants behind them. Use color to diminish distance by placing bright, hot reds, yellows, and oranges toward you and cooler colors behind. To lengthen the distance, place cool blues and mauves toward you and subdued pastels in the back.

Landscaping Tip:

Use foliage shape, size, texture, and color to manipulate the illusion of distance or closeness in the tight confines of a side yard.

SUSPENDING THE STRAIGHT AND NARROW

Consider interrupting the straight line of a path by installing a concrete trough that forces the path to go around it. The English have made an art of planting miniature gardens in concrete troughs, and they can be very effective. Troughs require good drainage, but once that is achieved, they can hold treasures such as succulents and cacti, and plants that trail over the edge such as Dittany of Crete.

Farther along the path, set down stones across a small river of stones. Then have downspouts from the house gutters and French drains along the foundation drain into the "river."

Create the river of stones by digging out a shallow swale that slopes slightly from the foundation to the other edge of the yard. Line it with thick black plastic, and fill it with river cobbles measuring at least 2 to 3 inches across. Choose cobbles that are heavy enough not to wash away during torrential rains. The stones should hide the plastic lining completely. Be sure this little river meanders and does not run in a straight line.

Place stepping-stones across the river or build a small footbridge. To heighten the effect of a riverbank, plant softly nodding grasses and slender-leaved plants along the bank. Also plant flowering shrubs such as quince, spirea, and witch hazel.

The movement of water is suggested by this "river of stones" in a dry side yard. Blue gravel represents water and crushed light gravel suggests the riverbank. Simplicity and an artistic arrangement of the elements make this a classic example of garden art.

A few water plants are quite happy growing in a tub of water set on the side patio.

Landscaping Tip:

Give the impression of water by creating dry creeks and placing water plants in easy-to-install containers.

Because rivers are associated with sand and gravel bars, substitute sand or fine pea gravel for a few areas you might otherwise plant with ground covers. As with the river of stones, underlay the sand or gravel with thick plastic to prevent weeds.

If you want rain to water the soil, use tough, nonrotting landscape fabric; it also will prevent weeds. Be sure to underlay the sand or gravel areas with weed protection. If weeds grow, you'll pull soil up into the sand and gravel when you pull up the weeds, resulting in more weed problems down the road and the eventual disappearance of the sand or gravel beneath the surface of the soil.

COLOR AND TEXTURE

Vary the colors and textures in your garden by using grasses, ground covers, mulches such as shredded bark or cocoa bean hulls, sand, gravel, and stones. Such variety also produces an effective counterpoint to all-green plantings.

Tall *Miscanthus sinensis* 'Giganteus' is a very hardy, 15-foot-tall ornamental grass that forms a well-behaved clump and makes a perfect backdrop for plants along a river of stones. You could easily build up a series of grasses, from low *Pennisetum* along the

CONTAINER WATER GARDENS

The side yard may also be the place to sink half barrels into the ground to within a couple of inches of their rims. Fill the barrels with water and plant them with water lilies if they get enough sun to promote flowering. A couple of goldfish will keep mosquitoes from breeding in the water. These water gardens are especially attractive at the edge of the river of stones, set half in the river and half in the bank. Or, you could set one entirely in the river to make an island of water in a river of stone.

A large expanse of lawn along the side of the house can be broken up with an island bed. This dramatic example uses strong vertical grass, salvia, and yellow flower spikes of verbascum to offset the horizontal stretch of lawn.

Landscaping Tip:

Hide the sight of the back yard from the side yard by using a barrier.

This attractive fence at the back of the brick side-yard patio narrows the path to the gate before releasing it to the back yard, keeping both parts of the property discreetly separate.

A lattice fence separates the side yard from the back yard and provides a place to grow a favorite vine.

river's bank to taller *Miscanthus sinensis* 'Gracillimus' and 'Zebrinus' before reaching the 'Giganteus.' 'Giganteus' has other fine landscaping uses in a side yard. It can spill out from one side of the yard, partially obscuring what lies beyond and softening the

hard architectural edges of the fence or house wall. It is particularly attractive planted at a corner. Elements such as this imposing grass also can steer the path into, around, and over obstacles and features that create interest.

PLANTING A FENCE

To decorate a fence, consider one of the hardy kiwis. They produce small fruit, and some have beautifully variegated leaves of green, milky white, and pink. Kiwis are vigorous growers and can cover a long length of fencing in just a few seasons. To soften their vigorous growth with a fine-textured appearance, pair various clematis with the kiwis. Choose such species as *Clematis montana,* which explodes into lovely, profuse pink bloom in spring.

When you use vines to trail along the top of a fence and spill over, match this tumbling movement with tall plants that grow up from the bottom of the fence. An exquisite combination is *Clematis macropetala* and *Kerria japonica.* The violet clematis hangs in masses from vines strung along a fence, then meets the rich yellow-orange flower balls that crown the long green stems of *Kerria japonica.*

CREATING BARRIERS

The final view down the length of the path toward the back yard should be of a barrier— a tall hedge, a fence, or a large evergreen shrub. This is more effective in keeping the side yard discrete than if the view opens into the back yard and gives away all its treasures.

The pathway swings around the side yard to a fence that blocks the view of neighboring properties, giving this garden privacy and protection.

THE SIDE YARD

This side yard is hardly more than a narrow passageway, but good design with decking, arbor, and latticework fence give it multilevel interest and usefulness.

Landscaping Tip:

The transition from side yard to back yard is an excellent place for decking.

The barrier is an important element and is the place for a special feature, such as an urn or planter with a dramatic planting, a recirculating waterfall, a natural rock and earth embankment planted with choice specimens, or a combination of great interest, such as an elevated stand of *Helichrysum* from which a tall *Abutilon* emerges.

When the path approaches the barrier, it can turn sharply toward the house and end at steps leading to a deck. If possible, tie the side yard to the back yard with decking or paving that begins at the rear of the side yard and wraps around the corner of the house.

DECK THE WALLS

Beautiful gardens can surround an L-shape deck that wraps around the corner of the house. The gardens provide an exquisite view from the deck. This is a choice spot because the decking carries you into the garden for close viewing.

The edge between deck and garden can be softened and erased here and there by placing planters of ornamentals on the deck. It also can be accomplished by placing plants with rangy habits, such as cape plumbago (*Plumbago auriculata*) in the warm zones or mock orange (*Philadelphus coronarius*) in northern zones, beside the deck so some stems and branches fall onto the decking.

If a tree grows where the deck will go, consider building the deck around it. Let the trunk emerge from a hole in the deck. Over time the trunk of the tree will undoubtedly grow wider, so frame out the hole so that it can be widened as the tree grows. Although a tree-through-the-deck motif is common, it is attractive and conveys a sense of fun as well

Brick and stone give character to the transition between the side yard and the back yard of this house. Red maple leaves echo the color of the bricks.

as respect for the tree. A tree growing out of the deck also ties the decking to the surrounding garden.

CHOOSING PLANTS

Because you'll be looking down at the plants near the deck, choose flowers with upturned faces, such as shasta daisies, pastel yarrows, eupatorium, and hybrid tea roses. Plantings behind these should be staggered, with the tallest plants at the back. Vary foliage type and color for the best effect, and make bold statements with attention-getters such as the purple smoke bush (*Cotinus coggygria* 'Royal Purple'). Repeat shrubs and standout plants

Strong colors and shapes are set against a stark white wall for dramatic visual appeal. This California garden affords the home-owners a colorful show from inside the house and out.

THE SIDE YARD

This climb takes visitors from the formality of the front garden to the play and rest areas of the elevated back yard. It is enlivened with pink and red Phlox paniculata *and gold* Rudbeckia fulgida.

in several places in the garden. This helps tie it together from all the angles offered by the deck.

Because the deck takes you out into the garden, place near the deck several plants that are fragrant or release fragrance when they are touched or rubbed. If your climate supports them, night-blooming fragrant plants such as jasmine or beauties such as moonflowers are good choices for the side of a well-used deck. Also consider placing fruit-bearing plants within easy reach of the deck.

The side yard takes you from the formality of the front garden to the relaxed, utilitarian joys of the back yard. Imagination, adventure, and beauty unbounded by the formal constraints of landscaping can rule.

The ideas presented here are designed to start you thinking of ways you can transform your side yard into a place of fun and mystery. Give your imagination and sense of fun and play a free rein in this small space. You may find that the once-forgotten side yard is your favorite place to visit.

Think of the side yard as a place for fun, and you may dream up something as theatrical as this Spanish-style fantasy (right) with its restrained use of plants and expert mix of straight and curved forms.

A stately, formal, and exquisitely lovely transition from side and back yard to a wooded area (left) is achieved with ferns and simple stone walls topped with Lamium maculatum 'Beacon Silver' as a ground cover. The tree trunks give the effect of columns.

45

THE BACK YARD

Landscaping Tip:
Create a wide back door and transition area that blurs the distinction between indoors and out.

The inside of this house flows out the back door onto the brick patio, greatly expanding the living space during pleasant weather.

Landscaping back yards can involve more than the creation of beautiful ornamental gardens. Busy homeowners have a variety of needs and desires they want their yards to fulfill. Even a small back yard can perform many roles if the landscape is well planned.

The place to begin is at the back door. In fact, you can even begin inside the back door. Just as foundation plantings tie the house to the landscape, details around the back door can tie the inside of the house to the immediate outside. For example, you can widen an ordinary back door into French doors that swing open in good weather. Pave the floor immediately inside the doors with tiles, flagstones, or other weatherproof materials that continue across the threshold to the patio outdoors.

A formal arrangement of paving bricks and brick-red paint on the back door makes a smooth transition from the interior to the exterior of this house.

Instead of a small back door that opens onto a cramped stoop, widen the area by extending cross-threshold materials outside to at least three times the width of the door. Extend the materials into the back yard so the length of the paving equals the width. If the back door is at ground level, the transitional area may step down slightly to a larger patio. If the door is several feet above the ground, the cross-threshold materials could lead to a deck that runs along the back to the side yard or to an elevated patio.

Potted plants inside the new doorway can be echoed by plants in containers outside,

and by other plants in the ground beyond. Look for ways outside to duplicate architectural details of the house. If there's a brick wall inside, for example, repeat it outside by building a wall along one side of the patio.

A wrought-iron railing inside may be echoed outside. A series of cabinets and drawers on the inside wall beside the back door can be continued outside as weatherproof cabinetry with a built-in sink, serving areas, and even refrigeration, giving

This old-fashioned back porch was designed to create ample living space outside. It serves as a trellis for roses and a place for potted plants that ease the transition from the house to the back garden.

49

the space a luxurious feeling and a kitchen function. In such ways, the space inside and outside the back door becomes one contiguous area that can be closed off in cold or inclement weather.

Plants in assorted containers bring the garden onto this back porch, creating an inviting space for relaxation. The expanse of glass extends the garden effect inside the house as well.

■ Place for drying clothes
■ Outdoor sports area
■ Tennis courts
■ Doghouse and fenced-in area for a pet
■ Potting shed
■ Tool shed
■ Wildlife habitat

PATIOS AND DECKS

When you leave the transitional space, you'll want to encounter a patio or deck for dining and lounging outside. You won't want a long walk from the kitchen to a patio, however. Furnish this space with tables and chairs, chaise longues, or built-in banquettes for a

Well-designed back yard spaces such as this pretty patio give you the comforts of home under wide-open skies. The natural colors of the wood and brick and the profusion of plants tie the house to the patio.

Most outdoor fun at home occurs in the back yard. Here are some features to install there—each takes landscaping consideration:
■ Patio or deck
■ Barbecue area for outdoor cooking
■ Swimming pool and spa
■ Culinary herb garden
■ Vegetable garden
■ Fruit and nut orchard
■ Ornamental gardens, beds, and borders
■ Protective and ornamental fence

Landscaping Tip:

Include a place for evening fires in your patio area.

cozy, protected feeling. It doesn't have to be a large area, but because it will be used often, you should construct it with the finest materials you can afford. A practical rule to follow is that the more frequently you use something around the house, the higher the quality should be.

If you want to protect the patio or deck with an overhead canopy, consider making the canopy of materials you can roll back. This allows you to enjoy the warm sunshine on spring and fall days when shade would be too cold or dreary. In summer, you can shade the patio, increasing the comfort level underneath.

Canopy supports can hold vines, and the patio should be surrounded by plants that cover its edges with foliage. Arching limbs of trees overhead will add to the feeling of protection and shelter. Choose plants carefully. You don't want messy plants that drop detritus that must be removed. Avoid plants with special problems, such as black walnuts, which stain patio flooring; gingko fruits, with their unpleasant smell; and black locusts, which attract bees. Ask your nursery about plants that are beautiful, trouble-free, and easy to care for. There are many that need only a yearly raking after leaf fall.

For thousands of years, human beings have gathered around the fire for warmth, cooking, and protection. Including a fire pit in your back yard landscaping continues this tradition of the friendly hearth.

51

*A **vine-covered arbor flanked by white urns frames the pretty view down the garden path at tulip time. The frame emphasizes the view and invites exploration.***

OUTDOOR COOKING

Place a cooking and barbecue area at the back of the patio, so food preparation doesn't interfere with relaxation or entertaining. Installing a fire pit there also is a good idea. The pit can be simply a 3- or 4-foot circle of sand or concrete backed by a low wall of stone or brick in which wood fires can be burned at night.

There's something primeval, riveting, and very human about sitting around a campfire, talking or dreaming while gazing at the dancing flames. The smoke from the fire also helps keep insects at bay.

FRAMING A VIEW

Do you have a good view from the patio or deck? Frame it with large evergreen plants or dense, deciduous shrubbery; architectural elements such as urns, balustrades, railings, or small towers; or trellises smothered in roses. Site these framing elements at the edge of the patio so they also mark the transition between the patio and the rest of the yard.

Note where the moon rises and sets, and plant your trees or tall shrubs so they don't block your view. The sight of a beautiful full moon from the back patio is an inducement to romance and worth the cost in time, money, and work.

> *Landscaping Tip:*
> *A swimming pool simulates a miniature lake that can create a centerpiece for a naturalistic landscape.*

The spot where the patio or deck ends and the rest of the back yard begins is ideal for a barbecue pit or cart. This location is only a short walk to the kitchen, and it's even more convenient if dinner will be eaten on the patio or deck. On the other hand, it's away from where people relax and lounge. A rolling barbecue cart allows you to move the cooking function, making it more practical than a stone-and-concrete outdoor grill.

SWIMMING POOLS

If you include a pool in the back yard, place it in full sun to keep the water and the bathers warm and to allow for quick drying of both the poolside concrete and bathers. For purposes of landscaping, think of the pool as a small pond or lake and set big rocks into the concrete nearby to suggest wilderness. Fountain-shaped plants such as ornamental grasses are effective, as are pines in a surface covered with sand to suggest an ocean environment. Plants with horizontally held sinewy limbs such as those of *Viburnum tomentosum* 'Shasta' echo the horizontal plane of the water's surface, and muscular climbers like wisteria provide a vertical contrast to the serene surface of the pool.

One of the most effective ways to landscape a pool is to create a spit of land that reaches to the edge of the pool, or even into it, drawing the wider landscape into the scene. Set the spit with large stones descending to the water's edge, with low-growing junipers and small evergreens filling the spaces between the stones.

POOLSIDE PLANTING

Plants that overarch the pool are beautiful and tempting to plant, but they will create problems and extra work when they shed leaves and detritus into the water. As a general rule, keep plants away from the edge of the water. Any plants near the edge should produce litter too large to be sucked into the pool's filter. When planting trees nearby, consider their size at maturity. Trees may not reach the water's edge when young, but they might overarch the pool when they're mature, sending yearly showers of leaves and detritus into the water.

No poolside plant should have prickly or thorny parts that could snag swimmers or those walking on the poolside surface. If you

Nothing relaxes like gently swirling warm water. A hot tub is a welcome feature in the back yard. This one is framed by seating and planters.

A culinary herb garden provides the incomparable flavors of just-picked herbs in your cooking. Here, edible green and purple basils and chives grow among ornamental pansies, santolina, and helichrysum.

want something green at the edge of the pool, grass is a good choice. So are sturdy succulents such as hens and chicks, which produce little litter and are attractive in full sun.

CULINARY HERB GARDENS

The area where the grass or soil begins is ideal for a culinary herb garden. If the garden is small, reserve most of it for herbs, although you can grow small amounts of salad ingredients, such as lettuce, endive, and radicchio. Train cherry tomatoes to climb the deck railing or patio fence.

A culinary herb garden can be as small as 10 square feet. Cross paths through the middle, making four squares 4 feet on a side. Consider planting a fragrant shrub rose in the center of the crossed paths. You can give each square a separate use. Here are some suggestions:

THE TEA SQUARE

Anise hyssop (*Agastache foeniculum*)
Beebalm (*Monarda fistulosa*)
Borage (*Borago officinalis*)
Chamomile (*Chamaemelum nobile*)
Lemon balm (*Melissa officinalis*)
Mint (*Mentha* spp.)
Raspberry leaves (*Rubus* spp.)

THE COOKING SQUARE

Basil (*Ocimum basilicum*)
Caraway (*Carum carvi*)
Chives (*Allium schoenoprasum*)
Chervil (*Anthriscus cerefolium*)
Coriander (*Coriandrum sativum*)
Dill (*Anethum graveolens*)
Epazote (*Chenopodium ambrosioides*)
Fennel (*Foeniculum vulgare*)
Lovage (*Levisticum officinale*)
Marjoram and oregano (*Origanum* spp.)
Parsley (*Petroselinum crispum*)
Rosemary (*Rosmarinus officinalis*)
Sage (*Salvia officinalis*)
Savory (*Satureja* spp.)
Shallot (*Allium ascalonicum*)
Sorrel (*Rumex* spp.)
French tarragon (*Artemisia dracunculus* var. *sativa*)
Thyme (*Thymus* spp.)

A bricked square discourages weeds, holds extra heat, and makes a visually interesting frame for a mixed herb garden of culinary, potpourri, and flowering plants.

Sumptuous rings of herbs, potted citrus, and tumbling pink and white flowers are planted close to the patio, transforming a simple back yard into a miniature Garden of Eden for the homeowners.

Raised beds around the perimeter of this back yard save the gardener's back and allow for intensive production of herbs and vegetables.

THE SALAD SQUARE

Arugula (*Eruca vesicaria* var. *sativa*)

Salad burnet (*Poteria sanguisorba*)

Chicory (*Chicoria intybus*)

Cilantro (*Coriandrum sativum*)

Society garlic (*Tulbaghia violacea*)

Kales and mustards (*Brassica* spp.)

Mache (*Valerianella locusta*)

Nasturtium (*Tropaeolum majus*)

Orach (*Atriplex hortensis* 'Rubra')

Watercress (*Nasturtium officinale*)

THE FRAGRANT SQUARE

Bergamot (*Monarda didyma*)

Scented geraniums (*Pelargonium* spp.)

Hyssop (*Hyssopus officinalis*)

Lavender (*Lavandula angustifolia*)

Lemon verbena (*Aloysia triphylla*)

Pennyroyal (*Mentha pulegium*)

Rosemary (*Rosmarinus officinalis*)

You can add many other plants to the culinary kitchen garden: pretty flowers like true geraniums, coreopsis, and achillea; old-fashioned, just-for-fun plants like lady's bedstraw and lady's mantle; and herbs with few particular uses except continuation of tradition, such as costmary, feverfew, clary sage, and rue.

Culinary herbs frequently have pretty flowers—the clear blue blossoms of borage and exuberant colors of nasturtiums, for example—so the kitchen herb garden can be as decorative as it is practical. To make the garden even prettier, mix other flowers with the herbs, if you have room. Consider

Because the soil in these raised beds is enriched,
it can produce the maximum amount of food and
flowers in the minimum amount of space.

A mixed border of perennials and annuals beautifies the back walkway and screens the uninteresting area behind it from the view of people on the back porch.

Landscaping Tip:

Screen the utilitarian vegetable garden from the patio or house with flower beds.

VEGETABLE GARDENS

Vegetable gardens require deep soil, full sun, and good drainage. Because the vegetable garden is utilitarian, it is not always the prettiest feature of the back yard. This argues for placing it away from the house, toward the back of the yard. On the other hand, it needs to be close enough for the hose to reach and to discourage wild animals such as deer and raccoons from invading it.

Screen the vegetable garden with ornamental beds or walkway borders, so you see flowers or nicely chosen shrubbery from the patio rather than peas and carrots.

Another way to beautify the vegetable garden is to plant "field" crops that take up big chunks of space, such as corn, pumpkins, and tomatoes, in the back and other crops in raised beds that shield the field crops from the house. Devote every fourth bed to annual or perennial flowers, making a bold color statement that draws the eye. Or, set aside

choosing edible flowers that can decorate salads or dinner plates as well as the garden.

Besides those already mentioned, probably the most popular edible flowers are roses, squash blossoms, calendula, marigolds, chives, daylilies, pansies, mint, and sage. Although they also are edible, other plants generally are used simply to dress up plates. These include chicory, chrysanthemum, dianthus, hibiscus, jasmine, lavender, okra, pelargonium, sweet woodruff, and violets.

some portion of each bed for large, pretty annuals or perennials like sunflowers, hollyhocks, clary sage, and perovskia.

It's also a good idea when renovating a vegetable bed to allow the largest, best-looking vegetable to grow and flower, then save the seed that results. Sometimes even small vegetables can look extravagantly beautiful when they flower. A newly dug and composted bed set with small seedlings has a unique appearance when punctuated with a huge plant from the previous cycle that's flowering and setting seed.

When you prepare the vegetable garden, remember that rows and raised beds don't have to be straight. You can create attractive gardens by forming beds into curves. A round space for composting in the center makes sense, especially when the compost pile is surrounded by raised beds in concentric rings, broken by pathways radiating outwards.

Closely planted raised beds leave little room for weeds. The heavily mulched paths between the beds also suppress weeds. Vegetable production in this well-kept garden is high—although the spinach in the center bed is bolting and should be pulled.

If you have room in the back yard, a small fruit and nut orchard can be very productive. As these cherry trees in flower show, the orchard also can be a beautiful feature of the back-yard landscape.

FRUIT AND NUT ORCHARDS

The best place to plant a fruit and nut orchard is behind the vegetable garden, at the back of the property, because the trees become a miniature woods. Choose dwarf or semidwarf fruit trees so that all parts of the tree are easy to prune, spray, thin, and harvest. The smaller the tree, the higher the yield per square foot of space. Mix dwarf fruit trees with fruiting shrubs such as black and red currants and gooseberries.

Plant brambleberries such as blackberries and raspberries in confined areas. They tend to be invasive and can take over your garden. Limit them to 4-foot-wide beds so you can reach all parts of the canes to pick the berries.

A vineyard can be a very productive use for even a small chunk of the back yard. If you grow grapes for fresh eating, for jellies, and for drying as raisins, make the vines perform double duty by covering fences, arbors, and trellises on the sunny sides of buildings.

In the spring, you'll find that your apple, peach, pear, and plum trees are as beautiful as any ornamental. An apple tree in bloom is as pretty as ornamentals of the genus *Malus,* to which the tree belongs, and the fragrance of apple blossoms is deliciously delicate.

Although limited to the warmest regions, almond trees are also gorgeous in bloom. If you live in an area colder than Zone 9, you can still grow nuts. Carpathian walnuts, akin to English walnuts, do fine in Zone 6, and filberts grow in even colder regions. Full-sized black walnuts, hickories, butternuts, heartnuts, and northern pecans also can figure into the working landscape.

Envision a portion of your back yard as a woods. Instead of wild trees, the woods contain a tiered planting that rises from low

A large and vigorous Concord grapevine covers this arbor, to which a bluebird box is attached. In the summer the grapevine produces a cooling shade, and in the fall there will be grapes for jelly, juice, and fresh eating.

shrubs to dwarf trees to semidwarf and full-sized trees in the back. All produce fruits and nuts. Interplanting semidwarf and full-sized trees closely enough to shade the forest floor provides added benefits.

Clematis, grapes, kiwis, American bittersweet, Virginia creeper, and many other ornamental vines will flourish with their roots in the cool, moist shade beneath the trees. Their leafy, fruiting, and flowering parts will twine through and share the limbs of the orchard trees above. Plant the forest floor with shade-loving ornamentals like pulmonaria, hellebore, hosta, asarum, and other favorites.

Fruit and nut trees produce best when most of the tree is subject to full sunlight, so close spacing is a trade-off. You'll lose some production of edibles to create the woodsy

A cover crop of crimson clover under close-spaced orchard trees will be turned under with a rotary tiller to improve the soil and feed the trees before they leaf out completely and shade the ground.

Landscaping Tip:

Plant large orchard trees closely enough to shade the ground between them, and plant shade-loving ornamentals underneath.

forest-floor effect. In a home orchard, however, maximum production usually isn't an economic necessity.

Plant semidwarf trees so their drip lines will just touch when they reach maturity (about 6 to 8 years old). This will force future growth upward and create an umbrellalike canopy, under which you can create pathways. Most dwarf trees will reach a height of only 6 to 8 feet and won't be able to accommodate paths. Plant these small trees in groups to make harvesting and cultivating easy from all sides.

If you follow the preceding suggestions, a trip from the patio or back deck will take you down a path that runs past the herb garden, the vegetable garden, into the fruiting shrubbery, and finally into a woods comprised of edible plants. This path will offer ever-changing functions and varied horticultural experiences to those who walk it.

Don't forget to reserve space for the practical aspects of life: a clothesline so you enjoy the pleasures of laundry snapped dry by fresh winds and purified by sunlight; a doghouse situated so your animal will keep away deer, raccoons, and other unwanted visitors to the gardens; sheds and outbuildings to hold gardening tools and outdoor power equipment; a potting shed; a composting center; a play area for the kids; and a place to play touch football, catch, badminton, and other outdoor games.

The back-yard orchard or woods will provide food, shelter, and habitat for birds and other forms of welcome wildlife, but you also may want to plant special shrubs for the birds: They love the berries of dogwoods, viburnums, and especially Russian olives (*Eleagnus angustifolia*).

Russian olives are easy to care for, tolerant of most conditions, including seashore and drought; and grow quickly into dense, tough hedges up to 20 feet tall. Their density affords shelter and food for many sought-after birds. They make a superb screen or barrier hedge that is attractive in winter when it shows its angular, sturdy framework and flaky, dark brown bark.

Even a few dwarf flowering fruit trees cheer us immensely after a long, cold, dreary winter with their beautiful flowers and promise of sweet summer fruits.

An uninteresting slope at the back of this house was transformed by installing a rock garden and plants with many shades of foliage and bursts of lovely color.

Landscaping Tip:

Plant a hedge of Russian olives to feed and shelter birds. It grows quickly into a dense hedge, tolerates all kinds of climates, and is attractive in all seasons.

ORNAMENTAL BEDS AND BORDERS

In addition to practical elements, a back yard should include ornamental gardens. From the patio to the back hedging, you can intensify visual appeal with ornamentals. They decorate the utilitarian plantings and landscaping, and as separate beds and borders, they add oases of beauty to the back yard.

It's easy to see how ornamental plants with interesting foliage and lovely flowers, fragrance, and shapes enhance the functional vegetable garden or orchard. But when you plant ornamentals by themselves, for beauty alone, what guidelines should you follow for their placement? Here are suggestions for placing ornamental beds and borders in the back yard:

■ Site bursts of color at the yard's focal points: those places where the lines of sight and composition converge. To determine focal points, pretend you have to sketch the yard quickly using only four or five lines to delineate the major blocks of land and foliage. Your eye will be drawn to places where these lines converge. These are good locations for flower beds.

■ Draw the end of a long vista back into the landscape with an ornamental bed. Repeat the dominant color scheme of that bed in the foreground. The similar colors will tie the foreground to the distance. Subtle color changes that occur over the distance

The spirit of this lovely early 20th-century house is kept alive in the back-yard land-scape by the white lattice gate and fence (below) and the formal water-lily pond surrounded by a decorative flower border.

This back yard (above) ends at the fence on the left. Azaleas and rhododendrons in this area form a colorful backdrop for the more heavily used part of the yard in front of the wooden seating.

65

Ornamental plants occupy two-thirds of this back yard and grass one-third (to provide access and vistas). Stone walls and plant shapes, colors, and textures produce an artfully executed design.

will be heightened. If you use bright pink phlox in the foreground and repeat it at the end of a 100-foot vista, the distant color will be slightly less vibrant, accentuating the distance and making it more legible.

■ Accent turns in the paths to make them more visible and to reveal the shape of the path. Incorporate beautiful flower borders along the curves of the turns, for example.

■ Choose ornamentals for at least one-third, and preferably two-thirds, of your back-yard plantings if you want the area to express a lush beauty. Nature lavishes her beauty on the wild world, and you should imitate her in your back-yard designs.

■ Define open areas with borders of ornamentals. Lawns, for instance, are very useful. Despite their lack of favor in the

In this subtle but artistic landscape design (left), paths and grassy areas form angles that repeat the many angles in the roof, gables, and porch stairs of the Victorian house. The flower beds border the walks in a pattern that leads the eye to the house.

current landscaping world, they should be part of every back yard that isn't devoted solely to aesthetics. Lawns contrast nicely with borders of interesting shrubs and colorful flowers. At least half of your grassy areas should be contained by ornamentals planted around the perimeter. The rest of the lawn may flow up to walkways or the house, or stop at a fence or street.

Two areas planted with ornamentals flank an expanse of lawn and draw the eye to the back of this house (right), producing a charming effect. Without the lawn, this small house would be smothered by close plantings.

Tall and variously colored evergreens and different paving materials separate sections of this in-town back yard, making it seem larger and more intriguing than if everything was visible at once.

The goal of good back-yard design is to create outdoor living areas where nature becomes part of the picture. Here (left) a dramatic border of red penstemons and purple salvia spikes invites the visitor to sit and savor the rich colors.

■ Use ornamental beds to help create discrete areas and provide transitions between back-yard functions. Plant beds tall enough to serve as a screen or hedge that visually blocks one section of the yard from another.

In short, the back yard is the outdoor living space during clement weather, extending your living quarters into the fresh air. Each area has a function. Each should be graced with ornamental plantings to create both a beautiful and a functional landscape.

Because the sitting area is on the porch (right), the landscaping can be rustic and wild, incorporating native grasses, ferns, and perennial flowers.

PART TWO:
PLANTING STRATEGIES

COLOR-
THEME
GARDENS

COLOR-THEME GARDENS

Here the color theme is white. The plants have been carefully chosen so that all of their color variations tend toward yellow, making a bold, coherent statement.

Although you can create a beautiful garden by harmoniously arranging herbaceous green plants, trees, and shrubs based on their forms and textures, most gardeners consider a color-theme strategy the most effective way to create a beautiful garden. To use color effectively, select a scheme that limits your palette but doesn't necessarily eliminate colors. Pick a color you like; then plan your garden around it. Add areas of related or coordinated color and some complementary accents here and there for contrast.

Use colors in proportions that enhance the chosen color scheme. For instance, equal amounts of saturated red, yellow, and blue will produce the Dutch-tulip-field effect: eye-popping masses of rich color—welcome after a long, dreary winter but lacking subtlety or a theme.

Red, with its strong visual impact, is an excellent choice to accent these delphiniums, which range from deep violet to white.

A color theme begins with a single color, off which other colors are played. Know the visual effects of colors before choosing one as a theme; different colors have different effects on the landscape. White and silver, for example, are highly visible, reflect the most light, and seem to advance toward the viewer.

Yellow, the most optically active color, doesn't work well for a garden theme because the surrounding green foliage contains yellow and the lack of contrast creates an uninspired effect. Therefore, yellows, like whites and silvers, are best when used to separate or accentuate other colors.

Other colors with visual impact are orange, red, blue, and purple. Use greens of all shades to fill in the garden and to form the background for your color theme.

Red and gold coreopsis (right) combine the colors of their companions—the vivid red of Lychnis coronaria and the gold umbels of yarrow—to make an effective group of plants with strong visual impact.

Light pinks, such as this Astilbe arendsii *'Rheinlandí,' stand out visually from the golds, white, yellows, and even reds around them.*

VISIBILITY

Pure, saturated hues are the most visible. Consider, for example, the brilliant waxy reds and yellows of Oriental poppies. Less vibrant pastel tints blend into the background. Although the intense coral red of the 'Fragrant Cloud' hybrid tea rose is visually striking even at a distance, the soft pink of the 'Madame Butterfly' rose offers a subtler, even more beautiful reward for the careful observer.

Pastels, formed by mixing a hue with white, are usually more visible than darker colors, formed by mixing a hue with black or a complementary color. The bright *Monarda didyma* 'Croftway Pink,' for example, stands out better than the dull pink *Astrantia,* the mauve hellebore, or the lavender-pink ornamental allium. An exception is the striking contrast between a very dark shade and a very light shade, such as the brownish red of *Cosmos atrosan-guineus* with light flowers and foliage around it. This has less to do with the colors, however, than with the eye-catching contrast in brightness.

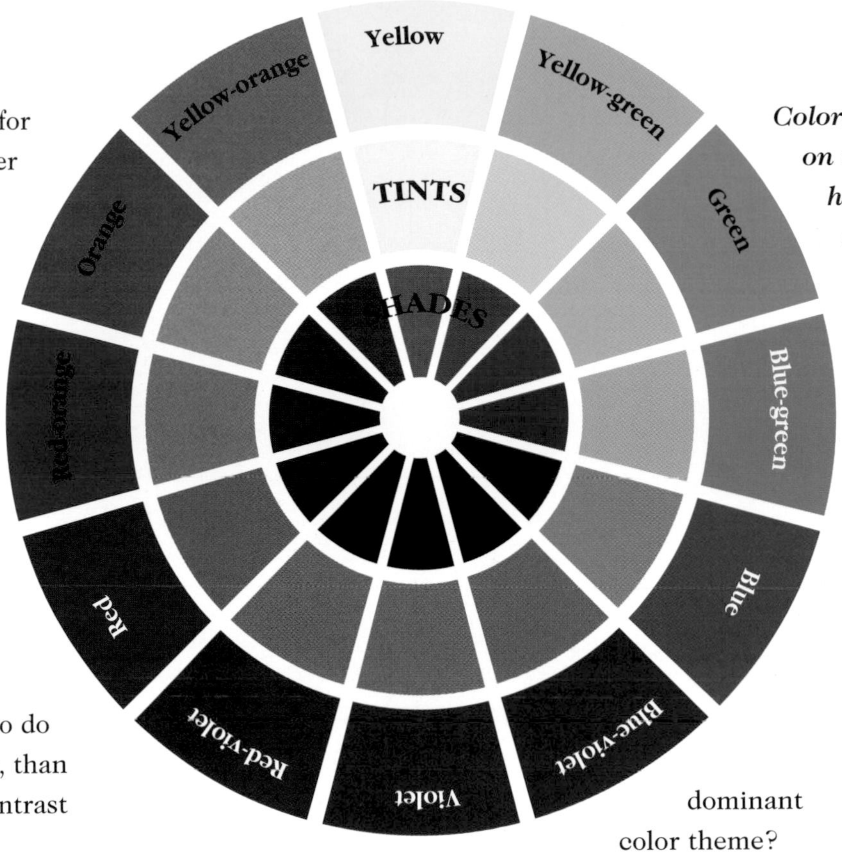

Visibility is important when designing a color-theme garden. You may take great pains to feature a large swath of blue flowers such as *Scabiosa* 'Butterfly Blue' only to find that its quiet, violet-blue hue is eclipsed by a few bright, candy-pink dianthus. Choose companions for your dominant color carefully, avoiding overpowering colors or an overwhelming number of them.

COLOR STRATEGIES

How do you know when contrasting colors are out of proportion, detracting from the

Colors close to one another on the color wheel harmonize. Those directly across the wheel are complementary colors and visually sizzle when they're placed together.

dominant color theme?

Plant two-thirds to three-quarters of your garden in the dominant color. These plants don't have to be precisely the same color. If the theme color is orange, for example, you can include analogous colors (those adjacent on the color wheel—see the illustration above): coral, salmon, red-orange, yellow-orange, yellow, brick reds, ochres, and flames. These colors are especially attractive when paired with plants that have yellow-green, copper, red, or gold-variegated leaves.

77

COLOR-THEME GARDENS

This striking color scheme employs violet and white flowers and silver-gray foliage in the formal beds, crowned with soft pink and white blossoms in the urn.

A blue color theme can include pure blues, lavenders, mauves, magentas, purples, violets, and crimsons, accented with pale yellow and white. These colors are pleasing with dark green, blue-green, gray, gray-green, silver, and off-white foliage, as well as with the violet and red-violet foliage of myrobalan plums and the purple smoke tree *Cotinus coggyria* 'Royal Purple.'

Here's a good rule to follow: Colors from yellow through red on the color wheel (yellow, yellow-orange, orange, red-orange, red, and all their variations and pastels) work well together as a dominant color theme. Another appealing group includes colors from red through blue. Pastel pinks, for instance, make beautiful companions for pastel blues. Foliage colors range from blue-green to yellow-green, so these don't ordinarily figure into color schemes for flowers.

White, lavender, mauve, and dusty rose-pink phlox (left) harmonize with related colors where they decorate these stone steps.

Pinks and blues make satisfying, restrained combinations. This delicate duo (inset above) features light violet-blue spikes of veronica and coral pink echinacea.

COLOR-THEME GARDENS

White azaleas, tulips, and spirea make a refreshing all-white passage in a spring garden. The varied sizes and shapes of the flowers keep this combination from being boring.

The colors between yellow and red on the color wheel don't mix well with the colors between red and blue. Don't plant orange next to purple, for example. The mix may be interesting and useful occasionally, but it usually creates a color clash. Displaying a bold yellow-orange *Kerria japonica* with a clear pink flowering cherry generates visual discord.

You can plant an entire garden of similar-colored flowers that bloom at different times throughout the growing season. The famous all-white garden at Sissinghurst in England is a renowned example of this approach. Choose any single color, from true-blue to magenta, but beware of monotony and be aware that each flower's color will alter with the changing daylight and as it fades.

Plant at least two-thirds of the garden with flowers of the theme color. The remaining flowers can be accent colors in soft pastels.

The more intense and saturated the complementary color—or color from outside the association—the less you need to accent your dominant color theme. For example, if your color theme is pastel blue, orange or one of its variants (red-orange, coral, or yellow-orange) would be the complementary, contrasting, accent color. If you support your blue theme with a pale yellow-orange, such as a 'Lady Banks' rose, you can use as much as one-third of the space for this accent. If you use a rich, saturated yellow-orange—a tulip or a ranunculus, for example—then just a few blossoms of intense color here and there are sufficient to relieve the sameness of your theme color and give it the necessary contrast. Otherwise a color-theme garden can lack interest. Indeed, it's the contrast that often focuses your attention.

Sometimes these bits of accent color can be found in the flowers themselves. Nature often produces flowers with more than one solid color or with contrasting colors, such as the bright yellow throats of 'Heavenly Blue' morning glories or the yellow-orange "bees" in the centers of red-violet 'Giotto' delphinium florets. Seen from a distance, however, these contrasts often disappear. Sometimes the contrast can be found in the foliage color or the stems, but again, this visual effect is lost at a distance.

The dominant color theme here is pale orange, beautifully accented by the burgundy falls of the iris and a few splashes of lavender and bold red.

COLOR-THEME GARDENS

The bold golden yellow of the black-eyed Susans (Rudbeckia hirta) comes forward to greet the viewer in this pathside garden. The lavender pastels and soft orange lilies in the background recede, giving this small area greater visual depth.

An accent plant can be used alone, but a group of three, planted in a triangle, creates greater impact. Using more than one plant increases the visual impact and benefits the plants' growth.

Pastels are good theme colors for small or back-yard gardens that are viewed from shorter distances, because paler colors often recede visually, which makes a garden appear larger. Bright, rich, bold colors appear to come forward and can make a garden look smaller, so they are good choices for a garden viewed from a distance.

OTHER VISUAL EFFECTS

Because most of your color-theme garden will be of your chosen color and its complements, the eye will smooth over small distinctions. That's why it's important to mass plants and to repeat the same color throughout the garden, tying together different areas of the landscape. Drifts of the same plant will seem to change color with distance, just as a mountain may be green close up but blue at a distance. This gives the eye the cues it needs to assess the true depth of the garden.

You can make a large garden more pleasing to the eye by placing pastel shades of the theme color toward the front, closest to the viewer, and by planting richer, bolder, more saturated values of the hue farther from the viewer. You might place a pastel salmon-pink flower, such as the hybrid musk rose

The roses (left) coordinate their pink, red, and white colors with the under-planting of annual impatiens, then are gone—but the impatiens will flower profusely until fall.

Red and pink tulips (above) create an early blaze of rich color in this quiet corner planted with green ground cover. The scene can be brightened again with annuals when the tulips fade.

'Nymphenburg,' toward the front of a bed, place a richer tint of the same color in the middle or back of the garden—perhaps a lovely salmon *Echinacea purpurea* 'Bright Star'—and the hot salmon-coral of an Oriental poppy or intense *Phlox paniculata* such as 'Orange Perfection' or 'Colorado' in the back or even in another bed beyond the forward bed.

By reversing this scheme and planting the bolder colors closer to the viewer and the pastel shades farther away, the garden will seem deeper and more spacious.

TIMING COLORS

Most perennial gardens are a snapshot in time—that is, the colors in May are completely different from those in the same garden in August. Any color combination will hold only as long as the flowers do—about three weeks for perennials. Your color-theme garden will bloom, make its display, and fade away as the plants go out of bloom.

This doesn't have to be the seasonal end of your garden, however. You can mix perennials in the bed so that a new color quickly blooms after the previous one, allowing several different themes in a single growing season. Many gardeners use this

83

Silver and gray strike the dominant color chord as they harmonize with the earthy colors of the large rocks in this dry garden. A few accents of pink and yellow are artfully placed.

strategy for mixed herbaceous perennial borders—mirroring nature's cycle of replacing spring wildflowers with summer ones.

If you want to create a color-theme garden that maintains its color for most of the growing season, you may need to plant the bed with annuals. These flowers take a while to establish themselves, but once they do, they usually bloom until the first frost. Ever-blooming roses and woody plants also are possibilities, but they usually have a flush of

bloom and then continue with sparser blooms through the season. Certain perennials, such as true geraniums and *Coreopsis verticillata,* will bloom for months and may help develop a long-blooming color-theme garden.

ALTERNATIVE COLOR SOURCES

In addition to using flowers, you can create color cues with permanent fixtures in and around the garden. A wall painted teal blue, for example, forms the perfect backdrop for the ornamental Scotch broom 'Lord Lambourne,' a choice cultivar with red and cream bicolored flowers.

Surround a rich red lamppost with pink and salmon flowers, or accent it with cool white and pale blue ones. The natural colors of flagstones or outcroppings of rocks also can provide color-theme inspiration. Another option is to paint nearby items in coordinating earth tones.

Coordinate bloom color with a prominent tree, such as a flowering crab apple or cherry in early spring or a mature yellowwood (*Cladrastis lutea*) later in the season. All of them feature beautiful masses of white or pink blossoms.

Flowering vines look elegant coordinated with the color of the building on which they grow. Lilac wisteria pairs beautifully with the pale gold 'Lady Banks' rose, and this combination looks wonderful set against a red brick wall or softly faded red porch. The many analogous blues of clematis, especially the pale blues, lilacs, lavenders, and red-violets, are stunning against natural wood or brick.

Foliage also can prompt a garden's color theme, such as the rich reds of barberries, the pink and white variegations of *Acer negundo* 'Flamingo,' the vining *Actinidia kolomikta*, or the low-growing *Houttuynia*. In spring the early foliage of *Pieris japonica* is a soft, glowing red that pairs nicely with the

many reds of the common azaleas blooming at the same time. The coppery-red new foliage of *Photinia fraseri* is another analogous match. At this floriferous time of year, the color palette, particularly its reds and yellows, is full of choices.

Foliage as well as flowers can create the color scheme in a garden, with the advantage that the colors will hold all season long.

GARDENS OF CONTINUOUS COLOR

GARDENS OF CONTINUOUS COLOR

A mixture of annual bedding plants such as these snapdragons and petunias keeps color going as perennials come in and go out of their showy times.

Most homeowners dream of a landscape awakening in spring to carpets of color that renew themselves throughout the growing season. Continuous color is possible, but your expectations must be realistic.

The only way to have a garden filled with color year-round is to hire teams of gardeners to move bedding plants in full bloom into and out of the beds on a biweekly basis. Otherwise, most of the permanent landscape elements—the woody trees and shrubs and the herbaceous perennials—have seasons of bloom that usually last only a few weeks. As a result, much of the yard will consist of green foliage for most of the year.

For the average garden to have as much year-round color as possible, you need to plant a variety of flowering plants, capitalizing on their different life spans and blooming periods.

■ Annuals add splashes of bold color and many bloom for several months, even up to the first frost. Some, like love-in-a-mist and annual silene, naturally reseed each year. Annuals alone won't provide the garden with structure or the range of textures supplied by perennials and woody plants, however.

■ Biennials, like annuals, provide bold colors. The first year they usually grow a rosette of leaves and develop sound root

Some perennials have long seasons of bloom, such as bright yellow coneopsis (Coneopsis verticillata) and violet balloon flower (Platycodon grandiflorus). Some varieties of phlox (Phlox paniculata) are also long blooming.

The dramatic trumpets and spires of lilies and delphiniums return year after year.

■ Herbaceous perennials are easy to enjoy year after year. They faithfully return after winter like old friends. Most have short seasons of bloom—about two to three weeks—with an occasional smattering of flowers thereafter. Coordinated carefully in the garden, they add harmony and provide staggered bloom throughout the year.

Choose perennials with long blooming seasons. Some, such as *Aster frikartii* and many true perennial geraniums, bloom shortly after the summer solstice and continue until the first frost. Before the solstice, nature steadily hastens its cycle of flowering, seeding, and ripening, in response to the increasing amount of daylight. Once day length peaks, the cycle loses urgency and flowering lasts much longer.

In general, perennials that bloom before the summer solstice have shorter periods of bloom; those that bloom after the solstice are likely to have prolonged periods of bloom.

structure. Some will flower the first year; all will flower by the second year and then reseed before dying. Canterbury bells and foxglove are examples of colorful biennials.

Leading the transformation from winter's dreariness into spring's bloom are such trees and shrubs as star magnolia, forsythia, ornamental cherries, plums, and crab apples. Ground-level plants include snowdrops and

Gardens of continuous color should always end with the bright display of chrysanthemums like these mixed varieties in a late-October garden.

crocuses. A host of postsolstice bloomers includes *Alcea rosea, Liatris spicata,* and *Aster amellus.* (See page 98 for a complete list of pre- and postbloomers.)

Gardens of continuous color also should contain a large group of late-blooming plants for an autumn display. The rich, autumn-color bloom of the garden mum *Chrysanthemum morifolium* may not show until October or even November. For the rest of the year it must take up space in the garden, adding another splash of green.

MAKING THE MOST OF FOLIAGE

Although every bloom has its season, garden space must be shared with plants not in bloom, so much of the garden is green for part of the year. With that in mind, choose plants for the beauty and compatibility of their leaves as well as for their flower color.

Leaves can be categorized by size, shape, texture, reflectiveness, and color. These characteristics can be contrasted or harmonized. For example, hostas, rhubarb, rodgersia, and acanthus have very large leaves; boxwood, cotoneaster, and erigeron have small leaves.

91

A marvelous color scheme emerges from a late garden that has flowers dying off. The color of the dried seed heads of the ornamental grass Pennisetum alopecuroides *echoes the color of the dried hydrangea flower heads in the background, while ferns give texture and goldenrod adds splashes of yellow to the scene.*

Varying foliage textures and colors catch the eye in this quiet shady setting populated by hostas, epimedium, European ginger, aruncus, and royal, Christmas, and ostrich ferns.

Leaf shape also varies, from the thin, threadlike leaves of coreopsis to the broad leaves of *Hosta sieboldiana*; from the deeply ridged, finely cut leaves of Japanese maples to the large, flat leaves of hydrangeas.

Leaf texture can be coarse, such as that of the rose, with foliage few praise, beautiful blossoms notwithstanding; semicoarse, such as that of a privet hedge; or fine, such as that of the grasslike tufts of sea thrift or the regular patterns of Jacob's ladder.

The reflectiveness of leaves runs the gamut from very shiny, glittery, and optically active (hollies and boxwood) to dull, light-absorbing, and optically calm (junipers, viburnums, and achillea).

USING FOLIAGE FOR COLOR

Foliage can provide colors other than green. Consider the white leaves of dusty miller, the silver of artemisia, the gray-green of lamb's ears, and the blue-green of hostas. Use variegated foliage with bands, stripes, and picotees of yellow, white, and coppery red. Some deciduous leaves can be red-violet, such as Japanese blood grass, or purple—a mix of cream, pinkish red, and green—such as *Actinidia kolomikta* (hardy kiwi).

Sometimes foliage is enough to make a color statement, as happens here when Phormium tenax 'Maori Sunrise,' with its swordlike leaves, mixes with grassy clumps of blue fescue.

Evergreens also provide foliage color. Junipers, cedars, and other conifers may be plain green in summer but turn into an array of subtle colors—gold, burgundy, or steel blue—during the cold months. The conifer *Chamaecyparis thyoides* 'Ericoides' is medium green in summer but turns an eye-catching burgundy-mauve when temperatures dip below freezing. Following are guidelines for combining foliage in the garden.

Contrast light leaves with dark ones: Display the brilliant gold foliage of *Lonicera nitida* 'Baggesen's Gold,' for example, in front of dark Irish yews. Insert a mass of light gray-green leaves, such as *Artemisia schmidtiana* 'Silver Mound,' among dark green and purplish-red leaves, such as the ground cover *Ajuga reptans* 'Atropurpurea.' To get a sense of the interplay of light and dark areas, squint while scanning the scene for overall impression.

Contrast foliage shapes: Using only large leaves can be uninteresting; combining many plants with small leaves can look too busy. Instead, pair a fine-leaved plant with a large-leaved one to contrast the beauty of each. The feathery leaves of *Paeonia tenuifolia,* for example, are enhanced planted beside a group of *Bergenia cordifolia,* with rounded leaves the size of salad plates.

Combine leaves of similar color but widely different shapes; or conversely, combine leaves of widely different colors but similar shapes. This provides interesting variation throughout an area, but the similarities prevent a haphazard look.

After you've considered foliage, choose flowers so the garden opens with strong color and continues to do so throughout the growing season.

USING BULBS FOR COLOR

Bulbs provide the earliest herbaceous color, beginning with snowdrops, crocus, scilla, and chionodoxa, followed by leucojum, daffodils, fritillaries, and tulips—to name a few common flowering bulbs. Usually by June these have withered for the season.

Bulbs look best planted in irregularly shaped groups, as though they naturally positioned themselves over a long time.

Red tulips and blue crocus announce the arrival of spring in the garden. Massing flowering bulbs, as was done here, magnifies their impact.

Bulbs and perennials coexist beautifully in this late-summer garden. The Asiatic and Oriental lilies aren't bothered by hot summer weather.

Some gardeners create this effect by randomly spilling a bag of bulbs onto the bed and then planting them where they lie. Or use them as the boundary markers for an area filled with the same kind of bulbs for a massed effect.

Many gardeners tie postbloom foliage in neat bundles. This practice is not recommended. It keeps light from reaching the center of the bundles, which promotes rot in wet regions. It also gives slugs, pill bugs, and earwigs a place to breed. The foliage should not be cut until two-thirds of it has turned brown. Until then it manufactures food that the plant needs to bloom properly next year.

A better solution is to plant bulbs where the leaves of other plants will cover the dying foliage. Perennials such as ferns and hostas

Color is coming from all quarters in this pleasant corner. Above, the trees are beginning their fall show. A careful mix of annuals and perennials enlivens the border that adorns the picket fence. Foliage colors, ranging from dark green through light green-gray, add their soft colors, too.

achieve this nicely in shady gardens. Try daylilies in partial shade or sun, or simply plant young annuals beside the bulbs. The annuals will quickly grow and cover the older plants.

You should always plant your favorite perennials, no matter how long their blooming period. Almost everyone, for example, loves peonies, although they only bloom for a couple of weeks. To extend your garden's blooming period, however, start with the following list of common, widely sold perennials that bloom for at least a month, and often six weeks or more.

PERENNIALS WITH BLOOM PERIODS OF 4 TO 6 WEEKS

March/April Bloomers

Helleborus orientalis

Brunnera macrophylla

Dicentra eximia

Polemonium reptans

Primula denticulata

Pulmonaria saccharata

Vinca minor

Viola cornuta

Viola tricolor

May Bloomers

Aquilegia hybrida

Armeria maritima

Campanula poscharskyana

Dianthus allwoodii

Dicentra formosa

Erigeron hispidus

Geranium sanguineum

Linum perenne

Phlox divaricata

Phlox stolonifera

Thalictrum aquilegifolium

Veronica officinalis

June Bloomers

Achillea tomentosa

Astilbe arendsii

Campanula carpatica

Campanula glomerata

Campanula latifolia

Campanula persicifolia

Campanula portenschlagiana

Centaurea dealbata

Centranthus ruber

Coreopsis lanceolata

Delphinium elatum

Dianthus alpinus

Erigeron speciosus

Filipendula vulgaris

Heuchera sanguinea

Russell Hybrids (*Lupinus*)

Lychnis chalcedonia

Monarda didyma

Nepeta faassenii

Penstemon gloxinioides

Platycodon grandiflorus

Polygonum bistorta

Salvia superba

Scabiosa caucasica

Sedum telephioides

Sidalcea malviflora

Verbascum hybridum

Veronica spicata

July Bloomers

Achillea millefolium

Alcea rosea

Asclepias tuberosa

Aster frikartii

Coreopsis verticillata

Echinacea purpurea

Erigeron hybridus

Eryngium amethystinum

Helianthus helianthoides

Hemerocallis hybrida

Liatris spicata

Ligularia dentata

Lysimachia clethroides

Phlox paniculata

Rudbeckia fulgida

Senecio cineraria

Solidago hybrida

August Bloomers

Artemisia lactiflora

Aster amellus

Aster spectabilis

Astilbe chinensis var. *taquetii*

Boltonia asteroides

Ceratostigma plumbaginoides

Chelone lyonii

Chrysanthemum parthenium

Helenium autumnale

Kniphofia uvaria

Liriope muscari

Lobelia siphilitica

Rudbeckia hirta

Sedum telephium

Stokesia laevis

September Bloomers

Anemone hupehensis

Anemone hybrida

Aster novi-belgii

Chrysanthemum morifolium

Chrysanthemum nipponicum

A newly planted island bed has only a small splash of color in the spring, before it gets going. Addition of spring bulbs would rectify the situation.

By midsummer, a few weeks later, the bed is filled with white, red, lavender, and yellow flowers, and reaching a color crescendo.

By early summer, poppies are showing red, and many other plants in the mix are getting ready to bloom.

By late summer, reds and yellows again predominate. Some poppies are making a return, and the rich brocaded colors of the late season are apparent.

The small pink and white flowers of erigeron bordering the brick walkway will bloom all season, as will the pink begonias behind them. A strong match, these plants provide continuous color while the plants around them open and close their color seasons.

To achieve an attractive mix of perennials with varying bloom times in a garden bed or border, group five to 11 plants of the same perennial in drifts (areas with thick middles and tapered ends) interwoven with drifts of different perennials. Repeat drifts of the same perennial in several places to give the garden greater symmetry.

First, place random drifts of the earliest bloomers. Staggering them rather than spacing them evenly creates a more natural look. Repeat this process with drifts of later-blooming perennials until the entire bed is planted.

Blooming periods extend from three to six weeks. Plan on flowers blooming in shifts: from April to mid-May; mid-May to the end of June; July to early August; mid-August to mid-September; and finally, late autumn to frost. As the flowers of one period fade, those of the next open. As you coordinate colors, keep this natural cycle in mind.

When the roses on the garden gate are finished and the delphiniums are done, this walkway will take on a whole new aspect as plants now in foliage begin to open their flowers.

While some roses have only a short season of June bloom, climbers such as 'Cecile Brunner' produce waves of bloom on a garden arbor all summer.

Even though you concentrate on perennials with extended bloom times, eventually all will spend their flowers and revert to green foliage. With many perennials, the foliage after bloom looks shabby. If this happens, plant annuals that you've grown in pots or elsewhere into the perennial bed to add color and to draw the eye away from the slowly failing foliage of the spent perennials.

If you buy annuals at a garden center or nursery, look for bedding plants that show no bloom. Nurseries often force annuals into a quick, early bloom to show color and to spur sales. This trick doesn't help the plant, however. It would do better to establish a sturdy root system and good foliage early in the season. Pinch off any buds you see on young annuals. When you plant them, pinch shoots and branches a bit to encourage bushy growth, especially if the plants seem too thin. To help extend the blooming period of annuals, trim off the outer third or fourth of the older growth. This will stimulate growth of new flowering shoots from their axils.

Some annuals, such as impatiens, produce abundant flowers and leave virtually no dying blossoms on the plant. However, many annuals do require occasional pinching of dead flowers to promote more blooms.

Structures such as pergolas, arbors, or trellises entwined with flowering vines and climbers lift garden color from the ground to a higher level. Choose from hundreds of climbing roses, including special climbing varieties of such popular tea and floribunda roses such as 'Peace,' 'Iceberg,' and 'Cecile Brunner.'

Clematis, sweet peas, climbing hydrangea, trumpet vine, and dozens of others provide ongoing color changes throughout the growing season. Some of the most beautiful flowers in the garden are on vines, as clematis 'Dr. Ruppel,' 'Nelly Moser,' or 'Perle d'Azur' will attest.

USING SHRUBS FOR COLOR

Of all classes of plants, shrubs offer the gardener the greatest variety of leaves and visual interest. In bloom, flowering shrubs give presence and structure to the summer garden of continuous color. They do not decay early, like most herbaceous plants.

Most shrubs bloom relatively early, but as with perennials, some bloom mid-season and later. To promote continuous color, try late-blooming varieties of abelia, abutilon, buddleia, clethra, franklinia, hibiscus, hydrangea, hypericum, lespedeza, nandina, osmanthus, potentilla, romneya, sambucus, stewartia, tamarix, teucrium, and vitex.

Most flowering shrubs are best displayed in isolated groups, especially toward the back of the bed. To interrupt the regularity of small, medium, and taller plants spaced from front to back in the bed, however, you may want to place a shrub strategically on the border or elsewhere for interest.

USING TREES FOR COLOR

Trees can contribute colorful flowers to the landscape during the year, from early blooming cherries and Japanese plums to the magnolias and crab apples of spring, followed by the late-flowering crape myrtles, smoke tree, evodia, and sophora, and ending with the winter-blooming witch hazels in the cold North.

In warm climates, many plants, shrubs, and trees bloom throughout the winter: Camellias, jasmines, acacias, primulas, violas, snapdragons, calendulas, and many others provide winter bloom where temperatures do not go below 20° to 25°F—a surprisingly large part of the country. (See the Plant Hardiness Zone Map at the back of the book.)

In whichever zone your garden is located, you can enjoy a satisfying sense of accomplishment when you create a garden of continuous bloom by carefully coordinating the foliage and flowers of available perennials, annuals, shrubs, and trees.

It's always a good idea to mix summer-blooming shrubs with plantings of azaleas like these. When the azaleas finish flowering, summer bloomers will keep color in the garden.

DECORATIVE
GARDENING

DECORATIVE GARDENING

Decorated with ornamental grasses, lavender, alyssum, and other plants, these once-plain steps are a favorite place in the garden.

Successful landscaping adorns the property with plantings that are ornamental, becoming to the home, and even striking. Successful landscapes stand in sharp contrast to houses sitting plainly on grassy lots and decorated with a few evergreen shrubs along their foundations. Where are the color, vibrancy, and life in those impoverished landscapes? A gardener is needed who can express excitement and joy through beautiful plantings.

It's fun to take an undeveloped property and transform it into striking grounds. But the benefits aren't simply visual. The gardener feels achievement and aesthetic satisfaction, and a sense of being privy to Mother Nature's earthy secrets. Today's home landscapers can transform even a simple one-story house on a small city lot into a place of beauty with the wonderful assortment of colorful plants that are available.

Consider a new rose that recently came on the market, 'Flower Carpet.' Before its introduction in 1995, gardeners seeking a decorative ground cover that would splash problem areas or featured spots in the landscape with trouble-free color could only dream of such a plant.

This sprawly, vigorous rose, the product of 25 years of breeding in Germany, has been successfully tested from Zone 9 in Florida to Zone 4 in Canada. It bears double, bright pink blossoms in large clusters for five to 10 months a year, depending on the zone. A yearly shearing keeps it tidy, and it requires no deadheading.

'Flower Carpet' has been called the most disease-resistant rose ever developed. It brightens the garden, adapts to containers and hanging baskets, and can be trained into a standard, single-trunked miniature tree shape. 'Flower Carpet' can do everything but climb. A rose with all these assets can be used decoratively to bring color to heretofore colorless parts of the landscape.

Many home flower gardens reflect the naturalistic English look of the Victorian Age—annuals and perennials planted in interwoven drifts of color in beds and

borders. The Victorian style, while popular, has not entirely replaced the decorative style that uses solid blocks and bands of color to edge walkways and lawns; to emphasize steps, patios, and decks; and to create distinct edges and outlines around landscape features such as trees, large rocks, pools, and terracing.

DECORATIVE EDGINGS

Annuals are especially useful for these decorative roles because many hold color from their first blooming until frost cuts them down. Those that have a flush of bloom can be encouraged to provide follow-up bloom by deadheading or shearing back. Moreover,

Decorative gardening extends to the brickwork in this garden, where the bricks form a curving, organic pattern that spirals in toward a pretty water feature.

Try to picture this wall and gate without the potted begonias. They add a perfect touch of subtle color and upward energy to an otherwise quiet garden scene.

annuals are often brightly colored, and bright color characterizes the decorative edgings of this style. The look is bright, simple, old-fashioned, and at its best, charming.

One of the best and brightest solid-color annuals for decorative edgings is the lavender-blue floss flower *Ageratum houstonianum*. It's low-growing, from 6 to 18 inches tall, and is covered from early summer to late fall with soft, feathery puffs of strikingly colored flower clusters. The plant likes full sun but tolerates partial shade.

The wax begonia (*Begonia* x *semper-florens-cultorum*) produces 1-foot-tall mounds of succulent-looking leaves and waxy

flowers. It takes full sun in the North but needs the relief of afternoon shade in Zone 7 and warmer. The small single or double flowers, depending on the variety you buy, create a busy-looking area of pink to red flowers.

Celosia cristata, either the members of the woolly cockscomb *Childsii* group or those of the taller, plumed *Plumosa* group, produce brightly colored areas of yellows to deep reds and maroons. Because they grow to 2 feet tall, they are usually placed back from the edge of a walk and are best bordered with a lower-growing annual of another color.

Dimorphotheca pluvialis produces many large, daisylike flowers, often with yellow and purple centers. The 'Dahlberg Daisy' (*Dyssodia tenuiloba*) is an underused and underappreciated annual that grows low (from 8 to 12 inches tall) and bears profuse quantities of 1-inch or smaller yellow-orange daisies with yellow centers.

Globe amaranth (*Gomphrena globosa*) is a neat 1½-foot-tall plant that covers itself in ½-inch fuzzy globes resembling clover blossoms. This plant likes full sun, blooms all summer, and is easy to grow. When the flowers are finished blooming, they remain as dried flowers on the plant for weeks.

Two kinds of candytuft (*Iberis amara* and *Iberis umbellata*) differ only in flower size. Both grow just 6 to 10 inches tall and cover themselves with tiny white, pink, red, or violet flowers, depending on the cultivar. They are long blooming and produce flowers from spring to late fall, and throughout the winter in warm climates.

In shadier gardens, *Impatiens* hybrids are the most popular annuals for decorative edging. They are available in many colors, including white, yellow, red, orange, pink, dark red, and peach. Once they begin blooming in late spring, they pump out wave after wave of cheery, bright color until the first frost.

Both edging lobelia (*Lobelia erinus*) and sweet alyssum (*Lobularia maritima*) are low-growing (just 3 to 10 inches tall). Lobelia's charm is in its bright, deep blue flowers, which are slightly larger than alyssum's white, lavender, pink, or violet flowers. Alyssum flowers so prolifically that it covers the leaves. Both start blooming in late spring and continue until late summer. Alyssum continues to bloom until frost.

Decorative edging doesn't have to be a little line of annuals by the path. As here, it can be a major feature, with clumps of alyssum and calendulas interspersed along the way.

109

Sometimes it's fun to ignore the rules of good taste and go for the gusto. A long, sinuous bed of bright flowers like these marigolds emphasizes the edge of the flower beds.

Cupflower (*Nierembergia hippomanica*) is another underused annual, excellent for borders and edging. It covers itself profusely with white or pale blue flowers from summer to fall, grows just 6 to 8 inches tall, and likes full sun to light shade.

Petunias in white, blue, red, violet, and purple are commonly used for large, splashy areas of color. Creeping zinnia (*Sanvitalia procumbens*) takes full sun, grows only 6 inches tall, and produces abundant small flowers that look like miniature black-eyed Susans.

The workhorse of the annual border or edge is the marigold (*Tagetes* spp.), with hundreds of cultivars available in solid colors of cream, yellow, orange, and red, and bicolored forms in all possible combinations of these colors. Their bloom is abundant and continuous if deadheaded. Plant them in full sun.

A summer bloomer, garden verbena (*Verbena* x *hybrida*) makes 1-foot-tall mounds of small white, pink, lavender, yellow, or red tints in full sun to part shade.

Pansies (*Viola* x *wittrockiana*) are familiar garden annuals that thrive in full sun to part shade. They come in many bicolor forms in just about every color imaginable. They don't give solid color effects, but they do provide bright, diverse color accents when they're planted with solid-colored flowers.

Low-growing (4 inches) to tall (3 feet) forms of zinnia have been hybridized to bloom in almost every color but blue. These sturdy plants like full sun and will tolerate some shade. There are so many forms that the gardener can select ones with the color, height, and habit needed to fill specific spots. They bloom from summer to early fall.

EDGING WITH FOLIAGE PLANTS

Besides flowering plants, use plants with variegated leaves, such as coleus; richly colored leaves, such as *Heuchera* 'Palace Purple'; and interesting colors, such as the mauves, reds, and grays offered by sedums, sempervivums, echeverias, and other succulents. Plant silver,

For decorative edging, the intense colors and long bloom season of annual salvia and zinnias are hard to beat.

Here they are contrasted with the prickly, steel-blue balls of perennial Echinops ritro.

DECORATIVE GARDENING

*A **subdued border** is produced by interspersing silver-leaved artemisias with trimmed evergreens and plants with contrasting foliage and quiet flower colors. The free-form stepping stones are decorative as well.*

blue-green, gray, and white-leaved plants (dusty miller, artemisia 'Silver Mound,' and santolina) to break up and separate areas of strong color.

When edging paths, walks, steps, flower beds, or borders with decorative plantings, you're limited only by imagination and good taste. Avoid a garish look by using the brightest colors sparingly and coordinating them with pastels.

If you plant the edge of a walk with lavender-blue ageratum, for example, low

mounds of orange marigolds behind it may be too strong. Both the ageratum and the marigolds are very bright. A more attractive alternative would be to back the ageratum with a subdued tint, such as pastel blue, pink, or yellow, or move to a secondary color in pastel, such as peach, purple, or salmon. Because lavender-blue and orange are complementary colors, lying opposite each other on the color wheel, combining them creates an optical vibrancy or clash. To soften the look of the border, choose a color closer to lavender-blue on the color wheel, such as light pink or mauve. You can always avoid a clash by choosing a white flower.

The longer the strip of decorative edging, the more strongly it will draw the eye. Use a long strip to emphasize a path so that foot traffic stays on it, or to highlight an awkward step where it may be overlooked. The bright, glowing colors of impatiens in a shady spot draw the eye to the path to be negotiated.

If there's no need to emphasize an area that strongly, break up decorative edging with shrubs or perennials, or by varying the colors and forms of annuals. By repeating spots of color along an edge, such as planting a marigold every 5 feet among ageratum, you make an optical draw that's almost as strong as a solid planting, and it will be even more decorative.

VERTICAL ELEMENTS

In addition to decorative edging of the horizontal landscape components, vertical elements such as walls, trellises, arbors, fences, porches, and porch posts benefit from decorative plantings. Climbing plants soften and enhance these elements.

There is probably no garden flower prettier than the hybrid clematis, with its 4- to 6-inch-wide multisepaled stars in the blue to purple range. Many exquisite cultivars combine pastel backgrounds with color-coordinated bars that run down the centers of the sepals. 'Dr. Ruppel,' for example, has pink petals and crimson bars; 'Nelly Moser' has pale lilac-pink sepals with a stronger color bar down the center, and 'Barbara Jackman' has mauve sepals with a magenta center stripe.

Sweet peas and cosmos strike up the color scheme of this pretty border, which dresses up an otherwise dull and uninteresting wall.

DECORATIVE GARDENING

Drifts of perennials and clumps of shrubs decorate a garden path. Rose canes have been bent over and pinned to the ground so buds grow along their lengths, not just at the tips.

In Zone 6 and warmer, *Clematis montana* 'Rubens' is a vigorous climber that tolerates most conditions except drought. Covered with four-sepaled blossoms and three-leaflet leaves in spring, it is incomparable for twining into small trees, covering arbors and trellises, and beautifying whatever it touches. The flowers are a lovely soft pink with a clutch of cream-colored stamens in the center and a barely perceptible sweet fragrance. This genus has many other species and varieties that also may interest avid gardeners.

Many favorite hybrid tea roses have climbing forms—'Climbing Peace,' 'Climbing Chrysler Imperial,' the salmon-pink 'Climbing Mrs. Sam McGredy,' and the recently introduced climbing form of the premier white rose 'Climbing Iceberg.' Some large-flowered roses also are climbers by nature: deep red 'Don Juan'; the decorative, multicolored 'Joseph's Coat'; and vigorous, pink-turning-silver 'New Dawn.'

Climbing sweetheart roses such as 'Climbing Cecile Brunner' are a treasure. They are extremely decorative, reaching 25 feet up and over a garage, trailing along a second-floor porch, and filling a side-yard trellis. Other climbing roses include the vigorous and sweet *Rosa banksiae* 'Lutea,' the famous 'Lady Banks' rose that produces masses of early soft yellow blossoms, and rambling roses like red 'Chevy Chase,' pink 'Evangeline,' and the species rose *Rosa laevigata,* which will cover sheds and trees with its long shoots and masses of 3-inch, fragrant white blossoms.

Many ornamental vines are suitable only in the warmer zones, but a short list of useful flowering vines for the temperate regions includes the trumpet vine (*Campsis radicans*), climbing hydrangea vine (*Decumaria barbara*), climbing hydrangea itself (*Hydrangea anomala*), perennial sweet pea (*Lathyrus latifolius*), honeysuckles (*Lonicera* spp.), silver lace vine (*Polygonum aubertii*), magnolia vine (*Schisandra chinensis*), Japanese hydrangea vine (*Schizophragma hydrangeoides*), and Japanese, Chinese, and silky wisterias (*Wisteria* spp.). Trumpet vines and honeysuckles, however, can be invasive and destructive to buildings and rock walls.

Some nonflowering vines also can decorate vertical surfaces, including Virginia creeper (*Parthenocissus* spp.); American bittersweet

(*Celastrus scandens*), which produces ornamental yellow capsules that split open to reveal orange-red seeds in fall if both male and female are planted; and ivies, although ivies tend to be a nuisance if they escape their boundaries.

Most of these climbers, and many others, such as the passion vines (*Passiflora* spp.), are suitable for rambling along railings and fences. To ornament doorways, take a tip from the French. Every farmhouse and country house seems to have a grapevine

Climbing roses smother an arbor over the steps in this lush California garden, inspiring a pink theme that's repeated in other plantings. The rich brown bark mulch on the path warms the setting.

115

Brightly colored nasturtiums spill over a stone wall and mix with a subtle but more plentiful planting of asters that also comes tumbling over the wall.

growing over the door. Try the variety 'Canadice' for its delicious seedless grapes, or an ornamental sort. Avoid the ornamental grape *Vitis coignetiae,* which produces gorgeous autumn color but is too vigorous for use as a small vine over a doorway. Grapes on an arbor, where fruit can be handpicked by those enjoying its shade, has been a standard approach for centuries.

SPECIAL LANDSCAPE FEATURES

Your property may have landscape features that you think would benefit from decoration—a prominent tree, for example. Gardeners sometimes build a low rock or brick wall around a tree, filling it with good soil, and planting it with hostas, perennials, or annuals for decorative effect. If you surround the trunk of most trees with even a foot or so of soil, the soil may rot the bark and destroy the cambium, the living part of the tree, underneath the bark. This, in effect, girdles the tree and kills it. To plant around a tree, leave a wide space so that the trunk is not bermed with soil. By all means improve the soil under the tree's dripline and plant it with flowers, but be aware that tree roots will consume a lot of moisture, so a regular watering program for your ornamental plantings is vital.

A mailbox beside the road is a good place for a decorative improvement, but keep these caveats in mind:

■ Choose plants that won't overgrow the mailbox, causing notes from the mail carrier asking you to free up the box.

■ In cold-winter areas, mailboxes by the roadside might be subject to road-salt injury, so you may want to choose salt-tolerant plants like *Rosa rugosa,* kept well trimmed.

■ Sturdy annuals that can stand abuse, such as marigolds, are a good choice because they won't overgrow the mailbox. They add splashy color all season long, and they are drought tolerant, which helps when the mailbox is some distance from a watering source.

Finally, you can have a garden that serves double duty as a decorative patch and as a cutting garden if you lay out flowers for cutting in bold swaths of color. Take cuttings here and there for the house or for dried flower arrangements . If you've planted enough, you'll still have plenty of flowers to keep your decorative scheme going. While you're cutting you also can deadhead.

Try making a cutting or decorative garden of everlastings like statice and strawflowers, and your plants will perform triple duty. They'll provide decoration in the garden, cut flowers for indoor arrangements, and a source for dried flower arrangements.

It's not just another plain-vanilla mailbox, with a miniature garden below, a flowering vine on the post, and yellow daylilies in the background.

COMBINATIONS FOR
PLANTERS AND
CONTAINERS

COMBINATIONS FOR
PLANTERS AND CONTAINERS

Pots are beautiful in their own right, even when nothing is planted in them. The two striated jars are fine pieces of garden art.

Flowerpots and other containers have a special beauty even when empty. The earthy colors of terra-cotta, the intricately sculpted cast cement, and the classic lines of well-turned urns and vases are all sufficiently charming to decorate living spaces. Plant them with favorite flowers or foliage plants, and they come alive. They also offer advantages not easily achieved in other ways.

A well-planted container is a work of art that combines the controlled forms of the pot with nature's exuberant flowers and foliage.

Potted plants can bring color and life to otherwise barren places such as decks, stone patios, window ledges, roofs, and interiors.

Pots and containers are usually portable. You can carry plants just beginning to flower to featured areas, then remove them when the flowers fade. This strategy is especially good for pots of spring bulbs, such as tulips.

The container limits the number of plants you can combine, which creates a dramatic simplicity of palette.

SOIL REQUIREMENTS

Plants in containers face problems that don't occur in gardens. Because the soil in pots is restricted, plants cannot expand their root systems and scavenge for nutrients. As a result, high-quality soil is important, and it should be replenished regularly, even annually. A rich compost is one of the most important ingredients in good potting soil.

The soil in containers dries out much quicker than ground soil and needs an ingredient that will hold water. Some gardeners use peat moss, but if it dries out, it resists moisture again. Better choices are vermiculite or perlite, two natural rock products that hold water until plant roots need it.

You can make fine potting soil by using 50 percent rich, screened compost and 50 percent vermiculite or perlite. The compost has been colonized by billions of beneficial soil microorganisms that resist raids by

As days warm up and outdoor living spaces are used more often, pots of intensely colored plants such as lilies, azaleas, tulips, and cyclamens can brighten plain earth-tone patios.

121

*Marigolds, petunias, and lobelia are densely
planted in this half barrel, creating waves
of summer color that spill over the rim.*

disease-causing spores and bacteria, thus protecting plants.

THE IMPORTANCE OF FERTILIZING

The best thing you can do for your potted plants is to water at least twice a month with diluted fish emulsion or a manure tea made by soaking a cloth bag filled with farm-animal manure in a tub of water. The fish emulsion is less work and mess. The manure tea is cheaper and easier, if you have goats, rabbits, horses, cows, or fowl on your property, and you use the manure in your flower or vegetable garden. Both fish emulsion and manure tea keep the potted plants well nourished, healthy, and blooming.

You can conserve a plant's moisture by double potting, placing a potted plant inside another, slightly larger pot. Lining a pot with plastic and punching holes in the plastic bottom for drainage also helps. Plastic pots don't dry out as fast as wood or clay containers, and light-colored pots retain water longer than darker ones. Small pots dry out much faster than large ones, so plant in pots that are at least 8 to 10 inches in diameter. Mulching the surface of the pot with an inch of small stones or decorative moss also may help.

REPOTTING PLANTS

When repotting plants from year to year, carefully brush the soil away from the root ball. Pry the white, tight, tangled roots loose with your fingers and tear off straggling bits of roots. Then repot the plant in fresh soil in the same container or in a container one size larger, depending on how much the plant has grown. If the potted plant has several crowns and your pot only has room for one, separate the crowns, each with its own root system. Replant one in your pot. Put the remaining crowns into other containers or the garden, or give them away to fellow gardeners, perhaps in return for one of their specimens.

Spring bulbs such as hyacinths, daffodils, and tulips are grown in plastic pots sunk into the soil behind the shed, then pulled up and placed in the pretty earthenware pots that grace this porch in mid-spring.

123

COMBINATIONS FOR
PLANTERS AND CONTAINERS

Marigolds and red salvia light up a plain corner of a side yard. The different-sized containers make a more pleasing arrangement than the dull symmetry of planters the same size.

PLANT GUIDELINES

When you combine plants in a pot, consider how you would arrange cut flowers in a vase. Plan for outward, upward, and some downward movement over the rim of the pot or container.

Some rules for combining plants in the garden don't hold for container gardening. In the limited space of a pot or window box, a riot of color, even clashing color, can be effective. Pink, salmon, red, orange, yellow, and gold begonias spilling from a hanging basket suggest fun, energy, life, activity, and anticipation. Deep blue lobelias look delightful there, too.

Foliage is as important in a container arrangement as in a garden or a cut-flower display. Consider the shapes and colors of leaves on flowering and foliage plants. *Helichrysum petiolare,* for example, trails its long stems beautifully through and around other plants in a container. It's also easy to maintain, because it tolerates dry soils if your watering schedule is spotty. *Helichrysum* commonly has a white, woolly form, but its cultivar 'Limelight' is a striking yellow-chartreuse that adds bright color to a group. A very large pot or urn planted with

Drainage is essential, so be sure the holes in the bottom of the pot aren't clogged. To help prevent clogged holes, place broken, curved pieces of pots, marbles, or stones in the bottoms of containers before adding dirt.

Because you feed your potted plants well, many will overgrow and become scraggly by midsummer. To improve their appearance and encourage reblooming, trim back long, woody, or scraggly stems by one-third to one-half. Pinch tips on other stems that are beginning to grow unruly.

The contrast in foliage types provides the appeal for this container grouping. Silvery, ferny artemisia, fine-leaved trailing ivy, and large, rich green clary sage leaves give a casual, blowsy look to an otherwise geometric corner of the patio.

Stocky pink pelargoniums combined with the upright, arching leaves of dracaena embellish a magnificent Chinese pot set in a lush, moist, semishady spot.

'Limelight' and a yellow-flowered maple (*Abutilon hybridum*) is a stunning sight. The lime-green *Helichrysum* spills out and down, and the flowering maple thrusts upward with big, papery yellow bells.

COMBINING PLANTS

Although you should experiment and use your creativity to combine plants in containers, there are some guidelines for making pleasing associations in large pots, such as those that grace a walk or patio. At the center of the pot place something tall and straight, such as lilies, the flowering maple mentioned earlier, annuals such as four o'clocks, or perennials such as butterfly weed (*Asclepias tuberosa*), astilbes, daylilies (*Hemerocallis* spp.), purple coneflower (*Echinacea purpurea*), bee-balm (*Monarda didyma*), or black-eyed Susans (*Rudbeckia fulgida*). Although fairy wand (*Dierama pulcherrimum*) generally is not cultivated in pots, try planting it in a very large one where its upright, arching, stiff leaves and stems, and gracefully dangling white to purple bells will be impressive.

Arrange medium-size plants around other plants so they fill in the rim of the pot. Consider annuals such as ageratum, cosmos, fuchsia, impatiens, coleus, diascia, edging lobelia (*Lobelia erinus*), *Felicia amelloides*, love-in-a-mist (*Nigella damascena*), petunias, and marigolds. Some perennials you could choose include baby's breath (*Gypsophila*), heuchera, hosta, nepeta, and English lavender (*Lavandula angustifolia*).

Around the edge of the pot, between the other plants, insert trailers and floppy plants that spill over the rim and trail out and down, preventing the arrangement from looking top-heavy and giving it life on all levels. Good annual choices include browallia, certain trailing fuchsias, geraniums, portulaca, nasturtium, garden heliotrope (*Valeriana officinalis*), and the many trailing hybrid verbenas. Begonias are excellent for this purpose in shady spots, as are the perennial bleeding hearts (*Dicentra spectabilis*) and Solomon's-seal (*Polygonatum biflorum*). One of the best perennials for container arrangements is Dittany of Crete (*Origanum dictamnus*). Its trailing habit is so pretty in a pot that it looks lovely by itself in a handsome container.

A few bright flowers—sweet peas—decorate a large terracotta pot containing an array of culinary herbs. Rosemary, lavender, basil, and sage grow near the kitchen door.

COMBINATIONS FOR PLANTERS AND CONTAINERS

Three dismal relics of the industrial age come to vibrant life with plantings of tulips and forget-me-nots—proof that container gardening can happen in any vessel you have handy, as long as drainage is good.

Marigolds, petunias, ageratum, rudbeckia, and Lotus bertheloti brighten a half barrel. Half barrels make fine planters if they have drainage holes.

In addition to the *Helichrysum* and hostas, other good foliage plants for containers are dusty millers, artemisias, ferns, palms, lamiums—especially 'Beacon Silver' (*Lamium maculatum*), with its beautiful variegations—phormiums, cordyline, purple sage, and kenilworth ivy (*Cymbalaria muralis*).

Roses, too, can be suitable for growing in pots, but choose carefully. The smaller-flowered shrub roses are especially good. For the classic look, train a rose to a standard and feature it in a pot by itself, or with a simple underplanting of a fine-leaved ground cover such as baby's tears, mother-of-thyme, or Corsican mint.

TROUGH GARDENS

The English are fond of trough gardening, an advanced art form on a par with some of the specialized Japanese horticultural arts. Troughs are containers that are usually rectangular, measuring 2 feet long by 1 or 1½ feet wide. They also can be round. Typically, troughs are made of cast concrete, but some are terra-cotta. Shallow trays with drainage in the bottom, troughs are easy to make at home. A well-planted trough garden is charming and adds variety and beauty to any outside space.

To create a trough garden, dig the negative shape of the trough into hard-packed soil. Place several 1-inch wooden rounds such as those cut from tree trimmings in the center hump to make drainage holes. Then fill the space with fresh concrete or cement. You may want to reinforce the cement or concrete with aviary wire, but be careful to position it in the wet cement so it doesn't show when the trough is finished.

When the cement is set up but not hard, pull out the drainage hole rounds. When it sets up hard, pull the trough upright, easing it from the earthen base. Then wash the soil from the center and the surfaces with a hose and brush. Use a steel brush to reduce rough surfaces.

The English plant miniature landscapes in troughs, using soil, pebbles, rocks, and plants, especially succulents such as aeoniums, echeverias, aloes, dudleyas, sempervivums, and sedums. Also commonly used are London Pride (*Saxifraga umbrosa*), baby's tears (*Soleirolia soleiroli*), and Scotch and Irish moss (*Sagina subulata*). Succulents, with their arid appearance, are best combined with other succulents or cacti to keep the dry-land theme. The many colors of the succulents and cacti create subtle and interesting combinations, even without flowers.

A rustic window box brimming with colorful geraniums and petunias enhances the charming entry to this house.

WINDOW-BOX PLANTS

Lovely window boxes can dress up an otherwise uninteresting wall, and they look attractive from both outside and inside the house. Fragrance is a consideration. Leave the window open on warm mornings and invite a fragrant scent into the house on a passing breeze.

Gardenias and jasmine are fragrant window-box candidates in warm climates. In cold climates, plant fragrant bulbs such as hyacinths, *Narcissus* x *poetaz*, and *Puschkinia scilloides*. Scented geraniums (*Pelargonium* spp.), Corsican mint, and many herbs take to window-box culture, where they may be reached easily and crushed to bring out their scents.

The main purpose of a window box, however, is color. Bring on the pansies, petunias, begonias, lobelias, alyssums, impatiens, pelargoniums, coleus, and celosias, which pump out color all summer long. These are the mainstays of window boxes.

Besides these favorites, consider globe amaranth (*Gomphrena globosa*). This hardy little plant covers itself in softly colored

pastel flower balls that last and last because they retain their color even after they dry. Some small daylilies are good window-box candidates. Flossflower (*Ageratum houstonianum*) makes fuzzy, bluish-purple flower heads that bloom all summer and into fall. They can be found in pink and white forms. 'Purple Ruffles' basil is a welcome change from the usual in a window-box planting. The firecracker plant (*Cuphea ignea*) and ornamental forms of wood sorrel (*Oxalis* spp.) are very decorative additions to the major players.

Many of the plants that make pots, window boxes, and wooden containers so pretty also function in hanging baskets. But here the ability to drape and cascade comes to the fore. Begonias again are featured players in hanging baskets. Kenilworth ivy hangs prettily and daintily from a basket. Sedums, such as donkey tail sedum (*Sedum morganianum*) or *Sedum sieboldii* also are exquisite in baskets.

Plant as many containers as you can comfortably care for. As every longtime gardener knows, you can't have too many plants in containers.

Hanging baskets and containers filled with flowers give this once barren and boring front entry a much-needed color boost.

BULBS
AND THEIR COMPANIONS

Irises placed along a garden path allow passersby to enjoy their variations in perfume.

During this entire time, from earliest spring to fall, some bulbs will bloom, providing a welcome fragrance in the garden.

WHERE TO PLANT ·

The first challenge in landscaping is deciding where to plant bulbs for best effect and easiest care. The solution depends on when the bulbs bloom.

You can plant early spring bulbs such as daffodils almost anywhere, except under the densest evergreens, where they don't get enough light. Deciduous trees are still bare at this time of year, so areas where they grow will get late-winter and early-spring sunshine. This allows the bulb to produce food, grow, and store energy for next year's bloom.

In these wooded areas, the spent bulb foliage will not be as noticeable when it droops and turns brown as it would in prominent areas, such as perennial and annual beds and borders. Therefore, interplanting bulbs with woodland ferns, hostas, astilbes, and other shade-loving leafy plants to cover the bulb foliage may be unnecessary. If a favorite path winds through a wooded, shady area, however, such interplanting will be more attractive for the six weeks or so when the bulb foliage is dying back.

Bulbs mix beautifully in the spring and summer herbaceous flower bed or border. They kick off the season with bright color while the perennials are just beginning to grow and the annuals are still getting started in pots.

The first flowers of spring are almost always bulbs—perhaps a clump of snowdrops (*Galanthus nivalis*) or a sudden bloom of crocus in a sheltered spot. Then come the mid-spring bursts of daffodils, irises, tulips, and hyacinths, and the blossoms of crab apple, cherry, and plum trees. Early herbaceous perennials bloom by late spring; then the annuals flower, checked only by our gardening ambition and our pocketbooks.

134

Bulbs aren't only for spring. Here lilies trumpet the arrival of high summer as Monarda didyma *(bee-balm) puts on its red crowns in the background.*

Bulbs such as irises (which technically aren't bulbs but are classed as such) work well as part of a mixed herbaceous border in early summer.

Bulbs, perennials, and annuals coexist nicely in garden beds. The bulbs find a way to pierce upward through the roots of perennials and annuals, especially in early spring, when perennials are just beginning to grow. When early bulb foliage is withering,

perennials such as peonies, daylilies, and grasses, which have early foliage, will hide the floppy, darkening leaves of the bulbs. Hardy annuals also can be set out among the bulbs early in the season, so their foliage covers the bulb leaves during decline.

Bulb Companions for Shady or Woodland Sites

LADY'S MANTLE. Use *Alchemilla vulgaris* for large bulbs; *Alchemilla mollis* is good for smaller bulbs.

ASTILBE. Besides making good bulb companions, astilbes are beautiful in their own right.

EPIMEDIUM. *Epimedium alpinum* var. *rubrum* is an exquisite shade-loving perennial that mixes well with small spring bulbs.

FERN. Suitable for shade, ferns of all types are invaluable for mixing with bulbs.

SWEET WOODRUFF. *Galium odoratum* is a quick-spreading and fragrant ground cover. It bears white flowers in spring.

DAYLILY. *Hemerocallis* species and hybrids grow well in partial shade and in sun, although flowering may be heavier in sun. They are an indispensable companion for bulbs in both situations.

HOSTA. The large leaves of hosta unfurl when the spring bulbs bloom, then they cover the spent foliage.

DEAD NETTLE. *Lamium maculatum* is a loose, vigorous, low-growing plant that blooms with clusters of pink or lavender flowers in late spring.

PACHYSANDRA. *Pachysandra terminalis* is a much-used ground cover. Slow-growing, it loves partial shade.

PERIWINKLE. *Vinca minor* is a tough, low-growing, vining plant that mixes well with all types of bulbs.

The big seersucker leaves of hostas and the feathery foliage of ferns are choice companions for spring bulbs as they grow to cover and hide spent bulb foliage.

Few flowers can provide the intense swaths of bright color that tulips create.

BULB FOLIAGE

Why not remove spent bulb leaves when they are unattractive? Because bulb foliage continues to photosynthesize and pump nutrients to the bulbs as long as the leaves are green. Cutting leaves off before they completely age damages the plants' ability to flower luxuriantly the next year.

Some gardeners follow the old-fashioned practice of gathering the ripening foliage into bundles and tying it together. This makes a neater appearance, but it has drawbacks. The foliage inside the bundles gets no light, and cramming the leaves together in spring, when rain is frequent, causes the leaves to rot and provides an ideal foothold for insects and disease.

Once the bulb foliage dries out entirely, you can remove it. If it is buried among the emergent foliage of perennials and annuals, however, let it fall to the ground and decompose there.

Although very early bulbs such as winter aconite (*Eranthis hyemalis*), crocus, and daffodils may be attractive when sprinkled around the lawn, remember that in most areas by mid-April, the lawn will need its first mowing—and this is too early to mow off bulb foliage. The only solution is to let the grass grow until the bulb foliage dries out, and then you'll be confronted with a mess. It's best to keep bulbs out of the lawn entirely.

By summer, bulbs and bulb foliage that dominated the early spring border are almost entirely gone. In this effective border, only a few iris leaves are still visible.

139

BULBS AND THEIR COMPANIONS

Although bulbs can pump out intense color, they also are effective when used with subtlety, as here, where white tulips mingle with fresh daisies.

USING BULBS EFFECTIVELY

How you arrange bulbs in the garden depends on the formality of your house and landscape. In formal settings, bulbs should be set in rows or blocks, or used as parterres. The walk leading to the front door of a columned,

porticoed house should have bulbs placed in straight, symmetrical rows on each side. Here the plain buttery yellows of daffodils would be too plebeian. Tulips would work best, especially if the tulip color scheme is formal, too: all white, for example, or masses of a single color.

Most yards are not this formal, however. They are tidy but not strict, relaxed but not informal. In such cases, bulbs can be used in curved beds and borders and on the sides of mounds and berms, building color toward the top of the berm, where a featured plant may be used. Azaleas, for example, bloom about the same time as spring bulbs, and the colors of bulbs on the berm and azaleas atop it can be coordinated.

When a bed is well defined— bordering the house, edging a walk, or set as an island in the lawn—a big display of a single kind of bulb is very pleasing. To achieve this effect, plant many bulbs of the same type very close together. If you are interplanting with foliage-hiding plants, space the bulbs close together in small areas, such as a couple of square feet, surrounded on three sides by interplants.

Try to avoid color riots. Aim for one-third intense and saturated color, one-third pastel, and one-third white. This will give you a soft, pleasing arrangement that is colorful without overwhelming the eye.

Informal arrangements of bulbs are usually reserved for locations away from the house, such as a meadow or wooded area. Here the natural look is best. Select an area where you want bulbs to show. Dig to a depth three or four times the length of the bulb from growing point to root end when dormant. If a bulb is 2 inches long, for example, dig a hole 6 to 8 inches deep.

Scatter your bulbs by the handful across this excavated area, letting them come to rest where they may. Turn each right side up so that the growing point is up and the root end is down; then replace the soil, which should be improved with compost, rotted manure, or leaf mold, and bonemeal for better bloom.

Red anemones and yellow narcissus add spice to the tiny white stars of Ornithogalum umbellatum *(star-of-Bethlehem) and the violet anemones.*

Many bulbs naturalize—they spread over time to cover large areas. Here a field of Chionodoxa *has found a satisfying home under the big trees.*

Lay a board on the area and step on it to firm the soil. Then move the board and repeat this until the entire area is tamped down. Now water it. When the bulbs emerge in the spring, they'll have a natural pattern similar to one sown by Mother Nature.

NATURALIZING BULBS

Many bulbs naturalize, increasing in number from year to year. Grape hyacinths (*Muscari botryoides* or *Muscari armeniacum*), for example, are exceptional naturalizers. Where they find a congenial spot, they can cover acres in the spring.

Crocus, too, naturalizes well, along with snowdrops, *Leucojum vernum, Leucojum aestivum, Scilla siberica,* and even some tulips. Naturalizing tulips include *Tulipa saxatilis, Tulipa tarda,* and *Tulipa humilis.* If given the conditions of their native land (the highlands of central Asia, equivalent to the high plains of the United States), these tulips will become perennials and spread. Other tulips that return year after year include the Darwin Hybrids, which are a cross between *Tulipa fosterana* and Darwin tulips. They have large, bright flowers and sturdy stems. Apricot 'Daydream' and bright

red 'Apeldoorn' are the most popular type of Darwin Hybrids. They prefer conditions similar to those in the Near East and Asia, which correspond to those in the Mid-Atlantic states, the center of the country to the Rockies, and the interior portions of the Pacific Northwest.

The champion naturalizers, however, are the narcissus clan, including paperwhites, jonquils, and daffodils. Daffodils are particularly lovely in meadows that receive a yearly midsummer mowing. They bloom cheerily in the spring, their foliage stays under the grasses and other herbaceous plants when in decline, and they are finished by the time the field is mowed. Under such conditions, daffodils can spread to very large patches over time.

When you plant bulbs for naturalizing, remember that in the wild, plants of the same species and subspecies spread out, making large areas of a single color. All the flowers in a naturalized group look the same, unless there has been an odd mutation. Colors, even of the same species, seldom mix.

Naturalized bulbs will be found in loose, anarchic drifts on hillsides, never as edging or in a straight line. And they'll occur in numbers. One hundred bulbs is the minimum for small bulbs; 25 is the minimum for large ones. Two or three times that many would be better. In smaller numbers, their displays get lost in natural settings.

The narcissus group of bulbs—daffodils, jonquils, narcissus, and paperwhites—are champion naturalizers. They can spread from small clumps like these to cover an entire meadow with their blooms.

143

Small bulbs should be planted where you can see them up close. *Puschkinia,* for example, has petals of white to pale blue, with darker blue-green center stripes. The flowers are tiny, however, and the stripes won't be seen unless you give them a featured spot near a path. Plant them in an elevated bed by a path, in a rock garden, or in containers on a patio or deck.

BULBS IN CONTAINERS

Bulbs work well in containers, and this strategy gives you a real advantage. If you plant bulbs in pretty pots, bring them onto the porch, patio, or deck, or take them into the house when they're flowering. Then move them to an out-of-the-way spot when they finish, so you won't concern yourself with the ripening foliage. Here's a way to do this: Bury planted pots in the ground in an out-of-the-way place where the bulbs get rain or irrigation water. Then simply pull them up—pot and all—brush them off, and bring them out for an annual display. When the

Lilies are wonderful bulbs that can be propagated several ways: from offsets at the base of the plants, from scales (segments) broken off from the mother bulb, and from small black bulbils in the leaf axils.

bloom is gone, return them to their planting hole. Mulch the planting hole heavily over winter. The bulbs never leave the pot, but you have their display where you want it as long as it is attractive.

You can feature a single bulb in a pot or mix different bulbs that bloom at the same time in a large container.

As bulbs naturalize, dig some up to begin new colonies elsewhere on the property. Treat them gently; bruises and cuts can kill them. Wash off excess soil and gently pull the bulbs apart, replanting them in new beds.

Lilies (*Lilium* species) are interesting and can be propagated in several ways. The bulb is comprised of scales, like a head of garlic. The scales can be pulled off and planted individually. Lily bulbs also produce bulblets, which are small secondary bulbs around the base of the mother plant. When these show roots, they easily can be removed and planted elsewhere. You'll notice little black seeds in the leaf axils of many lilies. These are bulbils. Like seeds, they can be planted but will take several years to flower. They are abundant, however, and can greatly increase your stock of choice lilies at no expense.

Chionodoxa is a cheery, early spring bulb that only grows a few inches tall. Very small bulbs such as these look good bordering a path where they can be viewed up close.

Many plants considered bulbs aren't true bulbs. Some gardeners think of iris as bulbs, but only *Iris reticulata* and *Iris hollandica* (the Dutch iris) are true bulbs. Bearded irises and other types are rhizomatous plants. Crocus, cyclamen, and freesia, although often thought of as bulbs, are corms. Dahlias and begonias are tubers, and anemones, cannas, and calla lilies are rhizomes.

Spring Bulbs for the Home Landscape

Allium aflatunense is an ornamental onion that reaches a height of 3 feet and has lilac-colored blooms in May and June. Plant bulbs 6 inches deep and 10 inches apart.

Allium moly is an ornamental onion that grows 15 inches tall and bears yellow flowers on 3-inch-wide heads in May and June. Plant 3 inches deep and 3 inches apart.

Allium neapolitanum reaches a height of 18 inches and has sweet-scented white flowers in April and May. Plant 3 inches deep and 3 inches apart.

Anemone blanda is the early spring windflower that blooms in April and May in blue, pink, and white. It reaches only 6 to 12 inches in height. Plant 3 inches deep and 3 inches apart.

Camassia species are May and June bloomers with blue, purple, and white flower spikes. They grow to 2 feet tall. Plant 8 inches deep and 12 inches apart.

Chionodoxa species, aptly named glory-of-the-snow, grow 6 inches tall. Their exquisite blue-and-white flowers bloom in March and April. Plant 3 inches deep and 3 inches apart.

Crocus hybrids are among the first bulbs to show lively color, with 5-inch blue, yellow, white, and purple cups in March and April. Plant 3 inches deep and 3 inches apart.

Crocus species, which have purple cups, are the progenitors of the hybrids and bloom early in March. Plant 3 inches deep and 3 inches apart.

Eranthis hyemalis is a tiny, yellow flower of March and April that stands just 4 inches tall. Plant 2 inches deep by 3 inches apart.

Erythronium species are called trout lilies or dog-toothed violets. They bear yellow or white blooms above mottled leaves in April and May. Plant 5 inches deep and 4 inches apart.

Fritillaria imperalis stuns the viewer with 2 feet of tiered beauty in red and yellow. It blooms in April and May. Plant 6 inches deep and 9 inches apart.

Fritillaria meleagris is the only checkered (mauve and white) flower known. It reaches a height of 9 inches and blooms in April and May. Plant 3 inches deep and 4 inches apart.

Galanthus species, the snowdrops, have 4-inch white, dovelike flowers and are usually the first bulbs to bloom in March. Plant 3 inches deep and 3 inches apart.

Hyacinthus orientalis is the familiar fragrant, Eastertime hyacinth. It grows to 12 inches tall and comes in various colors. Plant 6 inches deep and 6 inches apart.

Iris reticulata is a 6-inch blue-and-lavender iris that blooms in March and April. Plant 6 inches deep and 4 inches apart.

Ixiolirion pallasii freely produces purple-violet flowers on 10- to 14-inch stems in May and June. Plant 3 inches deep and 3 inches apart.

Leucojum aestivum blooms in April and May with nodding, scalloped white bells. Each scallop is tipped with a green dot for a charming effect. The fragrant plant grows to 15 inches tall. Plant 5 inches deep and 6 inches apart.

Leucojum verna is similar to *Leucojum aestivum*, but it is smaller and blooms a month earlier. It, too, is fragrant. Plant 5 inches deep and 6 inches apart.

Muscari botryoides is the familiar grape hyacinth. It reaches a height of 6 to 12 inches and has dark blue-purple clusters of florets. *Muscari armeniacum* is smaller and lighter, but similar, in its April and May bloom. Plant 3 inches deep and 3 inches apart.

Narcissus species include daffodils, jonquils, narcissus, and paperwhites. They grow about 1 foot tall and bloom in April and May. Their colors are yellow, orange, and white. Plant 6 inches deep and 10 inches apart.

Ornithogalum nutans is the 15-inch nodding star-of-Bethlehem with white, starlike flowers that bloom in May and June. *Ornithogalum umbellatum* is similar but smaller. Plant 4 inches deep and 4 inches apart.

Puschkinia lebanotica is a 6-inch-tall April charmer. Its bell-shaped flowers feature white petals streaked with blue-green. Plant 3 inches deep and 3 inches apart.

Scilla hispanica (*Scilla campanulata*), commonly called wood hyacinth, grows to 18 inches tall and produces a fountain of blue, pink, or white flowers in May and June. Plant 5 inches deep and 4 inches apart.

Scilla siberica is a smaller, 6-inch fountain of nodding, intensely deep-blue flowers that bloom in April. There is a white cultivar, but the charm is in the deep-blue species. Plant 3 inches deep and 6 inches apart.

Tulipa hybrids are the white, pink, red, yellow, orange, and lilac blooms so familiar in April and May. Plant 6 inches deep and 6 inches apart.

Tulipa species bloom in April and May, range from 4 to 20 inches tall, and have red, yellow, white, and lilac blossoms. Plant 5 inches deep and 6 inches apart.

A mixture of blue scilla and 'Keizerskroon' single early tulips strikes a gorgeous color scheme in a choice square foot or two of the garden.

LATE-FLOWERING GARDENS

LATE-FLOWERING GARDENS

An end-of-season explosion of color in the garden seems like a lingering party that bids summer farewell. Too often, however, autumn gardens have only a few straggling flowers. Annuals that bloom until frost and perennials that flower even later than that will bring color and fun to your garden until the end of the growing season.

In most of the country, there's usually a month between the first nipping frost and the freeze that kills everything. During this month, plants that can withstand light frost will continue to flower.

The end-of-season party usually begins in August and continues through October. Depending on where you live, it may last into November or even through the winter. Areas where plants flower all winter are a special case, however. In most of the country, the soft, sunny days of September and October offer the last chance to relax outdoors. Plan your late-season displays for areas in your landscape where you spend the most time.

White cosmos ('Sonata White') and yellow Chrysanthemum frutescens *(marguerites) mix amicably with silver foliage. Both flowers are familiar mainstays of many fall gardens.*

INTERPLANTING EARLY AND LATE BLOOMERS

The perennial beds that were so colorful earlier in the year will erupt again if you've interplanted them with late bloomers. Give late bloomers a suitable setting by cleaning up the spent foliage from the June and July bloomers. In June, you should stimulate more stems and, thus, more flowers by pinching the tips of chrysanthemums and asters. You should stop pinching by July, however.

Because masses of color are needed to compete with the flaming foliage of deciduous woody plants and because color cheers the landcape, when everything else is withering, consider devoting a perennial bed near the house entirely to late bloomers. During summer you can keep this bed interesting by adding annuals. If their colors clash with those of the late perennials, pull them out or coordinate the colors of the annuals and the late perennials.

Another strategy is to plant colorful annuals in the bed for the summer, and then in August transplant chrysanthemums from an out-of-the-way part of the garden into the bed. Even in late summer, chrysanthemums can be transplanted safely if you move plenty of soil with their root balls. This trick, however, won't work with most other perennials.

Late-blooming perennials also may be grown in pots and moved into a featured area, or you can sink the pots into the soil of a

colorful bed of annuals to diversify form and color in the bed.

VERTICAL ELEMENTS

Herbaceous flower beds present masses of color in low, horizontal bands, but the vertical elements of the landscape can be enhanced with late bloom, too. Many vines flower in the fall, especially in warmer climates. Vines carry flowers to porches, across railings and verandas, on pergolas and arbors, and up trellises against walls.

*Campsis radicans **(trumpet vine)** heralds the arrival of fall with its bright display of orange-red flowers. This vigorous vine is best trained on a wall its tenacious tentacles can't destroy.*

Annual vines that bloom in late summer include morning glories, which look especially good when combined with other climbers, such as this sweet autumn clematis.

Some common examples of late-flowering vines include trumpet vine (*Campsis radicans*), which produces orange-red trumpets in August and September in most parts of the country. It's hardy to Zone 5. A related—and superior—Zone 5 vine is *Campsis* x *tagliabuana* 'Mme. Galen,' which produces gorgeous salmon-red trumpets in the same late-season months. 'Mme. Galen' is not as vigorous as *Campsis radicans,* but it is better behaved, its foliage is prettier, and its flowers are showier.

Sweet autumn clematis (*Clematis paniculata*) is another showy vine to grow near the house. It produces a profusion of sweetly fragrant, 1-inch white panicles in September and October. If you plant it on an arbor or pergola, you can mix it with early and mid-season flowering vines for a continuous show of bloom all summer.

A more vigorous vine with white panicles is the evergreen clinging vine or tanglehead (*Pileostegia viburnoides*). It can reach 45 feet and tolerates light conditions from full shade to full sun. The vine, which blooms from August to October, is hardy to Zone 7. It is suitable on a trellis against a north wall.

Sometimes called the flame creeper (*Tropaeolum speciosum*), the flame flower is a red-flowered annual vine that is hardy to Zone 7. It has bright red, 1-inch flowers that appear amid bright green leaves in July to September. This Chilean native reaches only 10 feet, which makes it a good addition to a post or porch support. Like a clematis, it prefers its roots in the shade but its aerial portions in the sunlight.

A few vines that produce their main show in June also will bloom later if cut back to promote flowering. They include the perennial pea (*Lathyrus latifolius*), which closely resembles the annual sweet pea. It grows only 6 to 10 feet tall, which makes it good against a wire fence. Its flowers come in shades of rose, pink, and white. Woodbine, trumpet honeysuckles, and passionflower vines also will produce flowers through the summer and into the fall.

*The perennial pea (*Lathyrus latifolius*) will produce its rose-pink blooms again in late summer and fall if it's cut back after its main June flowering.*

155

A very hardy vine (to Zone 4) that blooms in autumn is the silver lace vine (*Polygonum aubertii*). It's a vigorous perennial with a loose, open appearance and small white clusters of flowers.

LATE-FLOWERING TREES

Another way to get vertical bloom is to plant late-flowering trees. Although they are rare, such trees are a wonderful addition to the home landscape.

The Korean evodia tree (*Evodia danielii*), native to northern China and Korea, reaches a height of 25 feet and is hardy to Zone 5. It produces clusters of small white flowers from late July into August, when few other trees are blooming. You may want to place it away from well-traveled areas, because bees find its flowers irresistible.

Also hardy to Zone 5, the Franklin tree (*Franklinia alatamaha*) is a slender tree that reaches a height of about 15 feet. It has unusual white flowers that swell to resemble large white marbles and open into five-

Crape myrtles (Lagerstroemia indica) *are dramatic late-blooming trees, producing masses of watermelon red, lavender, pink, and white blooms from July to September.*

petaled cups that hold sprays of yellow stamens. The flowers open a few at a time from August to October. The last blooms often open against a backdrop of long, lobed leaves that turn a rich leathery red to red-orange in the fall.

Crape myrtles (*Lagerstroemia indica*) bloom in August and September. These 20-foot-tall trees, hardy to Zone 7, fill with bloom from July to September in strong, varied shades of red, pink, lavender, or white. They can be single-trunk trees or can be multitrunk, tall shrubs. The shrubs are even more floriferous and colorful than in the single-trunk form. Crape myrtles are wonderful in full sun by a street or roadway, or flanking a driveway.

A striking big-landscape tree is the Japanese pagoda tree (*Sophora japonica*), which reaches a height of 50 feet. Mix the tree with other large deciduous trees that form a woodsy area. Its dark green foliage sets off pyramidal clusters of yellowish-white pealike flowers that appear from July through August.

The summer sweet (*Clethra alnifolia* 'Pinkspire') is a small tree (or a large shrub if it is multitrunked) that grows only 8 to 10 feet tall. The single-trunk tree can be underplanted with *Liriope muscari,* the perennial ground cover. The summer sweet blooms with lovely pink flower spikes in August, when the liriope is producing showy, blue-purple clusters of flowers.

The fertile flowers of this big-leaf hydrangea (Hydrangea macrophylla) are finished and have faded into inconspicuous clusters in the centers of the rings of big, sterile, pinkish sepals that can hang on the shrubs for months.

LATE-BLOOMING SHRUBS

Many shrubs are late bloomers. One of the best includes Scotch heather (*Calluna vulgaris*). Small, double,pink flowers crowd its many stems from August to October. It's hardy to Zone 5, and if your conditions are like Scotland's (northeastern U.S. coastal zones and the Pacific Northwest), it should do especially well.

The blue mist shrub (*Caryopteris* x *clandonensis* 'Heavenly Blue') is a small, woody plant that grows to about 3 feet tall. Hardy to Zone 6, it produces beautiful deep blue, fringed flowers from the axils of gray-green leaves from August to frost. Three to five shrubs edging a flower bed near the house make a pretty blue display during a drab time of year.

The familiar rose of Sharon (*Hibiscus syriacus*) blooms in August with showy cupped flowers in shades of pink, red, blue, and white. Although rose of Sharon can stand alone as a specimen tree, it mixes well with tall shrubs in a sunny spot.

The big-leaf hydrangea (*Hydrangea macrophylla*) begins blooming in July and continues until September with big flower balls of blue, carmine, pink, rose, salmon-rose, and white, depending on the cultivar. 'Nikko Blue' is one of the prettiest forms.

The bush cinquefoil (*Potentilla fruticosa*) is a low-growing shrub just 2 to 3 feet tall. It has fine foliage and small, pale yellow, roselike flowers that appear in June and continue to dot the shrub until October. Because of its neat appearance, density, and long blooming period, cinquefoil makes an excellent low hedge for an herb garden or parterre and is a perfect edging for a walk.

The Kashgar tamarisk (*Tamarix hispida*) is also a small shrub, about 4 or 5 feet tall. Amassed with tiny pink florets, it resembles

A choice friend from Scotland, heather (Calluna vulgaris) covers the ground with its soft, pink flowers into October.

From the end of July into October, chaste tree (Vitex agnus-castus) is a star performer in the garden. With its showy lavender flower spikes, the tree does best with plenty of summer heat and moderate watering.

a pink cloud when blooming in August and September. Hardy to Zone 5, this tamarisk does particularly well in northern coastal sites. It is chancy in the Midwest, although if planted in well-drained soil in full sun, it will grow in most areas. Cut it back to the ground after it goes dormant, because it blooms on new growth each year and is unattractive in winter. Mix it with shrubs in the side yard or at the back of the property, where distance will enhance its cloudlike appearance.

Called the chaste tree, *Vitex agnus-castus* is a fairly large shrub that reaches a height of about 10 feet. The shrub produces lovely 1-foot-long slender lavender-blue flower spikes from July to October. It looks a bit like a butterfly bush but has a more spiky appearance. Most beautiful when viewed at a distance, place the chaste tree toward the back edge of the landscape.

If you live in Zone 8 and warmer, you will find other trees, shrubs, and vines that bloom late and even throughout the winter. For cold-winter zones (Zone 7 and colder), however, these are the mainstays.

FALL-BLOOMING BULBS

Bulbs usually bloom in the spring, but a number of them bloom in the fall. Dahlias, especially, enrich the fall landscape with their hot colors. Tall hybrid dahlias reach a height of 5 feet and carry huge, 1-foot-wide, daisylike double flowers. They are stars in the mixed border and grow well in pots. Their fiery colors are unmatched; they are also available in pastels. New dahlias grown from seed are treated as annual bedding plants and reach only a foot or two in height.

Cannas, which have large, dark, coarse foliage and intense colors, bloom until the first frost. Although they frequently star in island beds, they are best sited in a mixed planting. For fragrance, plant tuberoses near the porch or patio, especially 'Early Mexican,' which flowers in September. 'The Pearl' is a white, double tuberose with an intoxicating scent that blooms from July through September.

Fragrant naked ladies (*Amaryllis belladona*) bloom in late summer, after the leaves have died. Many gardeners mix the bulb with chrysanthemums to hide the naked stems and provide follow-up color after the ladies have died.

After a summer's worth of heat, cannas open their showy flowers in time for fall. These pink cannas make a cheery partner for the marigolds.

161

The autumn crocus (*Colchicum autumnale*) blossoms in mid-fall and looks very much like the spring crocus, with flowers of mauve, pink, rose, purple, violet, amethyst, and white. It's larger, however, and reaches a height of 8 inches. The so-called winter daffodil (*Sternbergia lutea*) produces four or five yellow crocuslike flowers from each bulb in the fall, which last until frost. In addition, some true crocuses bloom in fall, including *Crocus kotschyanus, Crocus sativus* (the saffron crocus), and *Crocus speciosus.*

Begonias, both tuberous and fibrous-rooted, like the cool fall weather and bloom until frost. Tuberous begonias are beautiful in hanging pots on the porch, and fibrous-rooted varieties are perfect for bedding near the house.

The magic lily (*Lycoris squamigera*) acts much like the naked lady. Its leaves die down by fall and 24-inch, fragrant, rose-colored trumpets appear that are fringed with amethyst blue.

The leaves of Colchicum autumnale *(meadow saffron) have long since withered, when it sends up its pink flowers in September.*

COLORFUL FALL ANNUALS

Many annuals, such as impatiens, flower bravely through the summer and into the fall, but some are grown precisely for their fall bloom. Ornamental kales and cabbages provide colorful foliage even after the first frosts.

The familiar pot marigold (*Calendula officinalis*) is a fall annual. It should be sown in eastern gardens in June for strong fall bloom. On the warm west coast, they bloom all winter. Their bright gold and orange edible flower petals can add visual appeal to salads and color dips and desserts.

China asters (*Callistephus chinensis*) are excellent cut-and-come-again flowers. The more you cut them, the more floriferous they become. With an appearance similar to small mums, their lavender, purple, pink, red, and white flowers bloom from early fall until after the leaves drop.

Cosmos (*Cosmos bipinnatus*) are mainstays of perennial or annual borders, because they bloom from high summer through fall. Slender, willowy plants, they should be sown everywhere for spots of strong colors, including white, rose, red, and yellow.

Other fall annuals for the border and for mixing with fall perennials such as mums and Japanese anemones include garden balsam (*Impatiens balsamina*); sweet alyssum (*Lobularia maritima*), which blooms in early summer and again in fall; the ground-covering

The pink flowers of annual Nicotiana alata *continue until frost. They look good en masse and combined with other late-blooming flowers.*

Given a good pruning of spent flower trusses and midsummer feedings, many roses bloom until the first frost. In fact, roses in protected spots often are the last flowers in the garden.

FALL FOLIAGE PLANTS

Some plants offer not flowers but spectacular foliage color in the fall. Standouts include the shrubby fothergillas, Virginia creeper vine, and sumacs. Others bring colorful berries to the late garden: the mountain ash tree, *Cornus kousa,* and crab apples, with fruit that hangs on into winter. One of the best is the American bittersweet (*Celastrus scandens*). Its yellow seed pods open to reveal red-orange clusters of berries.

Lysimachia congestiflora, which produces gold and red cups that bloom into November; and flowering tobacco (*Nicotiana alata*), which can be mixed into a border, where it will bloom in summer and produce fragrant, white, red, or pink tubular flowers until frost.

All these plants, as well as the fall-flowering perennials that follow, offer an abundance of strong color late in the season. With a little planning, the last hurrah may be the brightest and the best of all.

Sumac, ordinarily wild and weedy, turns brilliant in the fall, producing what is probably the most intense colors of any of the autumn all-stars.

LATE-FLOWERING GARDENS

Among the most beloved flowers of the late garden, chrysanthemums sometimes bloom until Thanksgiving.

Here the plants are having a garden party—a last fling before cold weather shuts them down. At play are pink Michaelmas daisies, dahlias, geraniums, and many others in a wonderful riot of color.

LATE-BLOOMING PERENNIALS

Aconitum fischeri

Azure monkshood, also sometimes listed as *Aconitum carmichaelii*, grows 2 to 5 feet tall, likes partial shade, does best in Zone 3, and blooms from late August into October. Dark purplish-blue hooded flowers appear singly at the tips of the stiff stems.

Anemone hupehensis

Japanese anemone grows 18 to 24 inches tall, likes partial shade and does best in Zone 5. It flowers from early September into October. Soft rose-purple to rose-carmine blossoms several inches across appear on tall stems.

Anemone x hybrida

Hybrid Japanese anemone grows 3 to 5 feet tall, likes full sun, does best in Zone 5, and flowers from September through October. This sturdy plant has 3-inch, single, semidouble, or double flowers in shades of rose, pink, purplish pink, and white with prominent yellow centers. Many varieties are available.

Aster novae-angliae

New England aster grows 3 to 6 feet tall, likes full sun, does best in Zone 3, and flowers from late August into October. Several dozen 2-inch, daisylike flowers form in each cluster, and several clusters on each stem cover the plants with lavender, pink, and violet flowers.

Aster novi-belgii

New York Aster grows 2 to 4 feet tall, likes full sun, does best in Zone 4, and flowers from early September well into October. Pink, purple, violet, and white flowers with yellow eyes smother the airy, bushy plants. This aster escaped the garden and grows wild in many parts of the Northeast.

Boltonia asteroides

Boltonia grows 4 to 7 feet tall, likes full sun, does best in Zone 3, and flowers from late August to October. A big, shaggy version of an aster, its flowers come in shades of violet, pink, purple, and white.

Chrysanthemum x morifolium

Chrysanthemum grows 1 to 4 feet tall, likes full sun, does best in Zone 4, and flowers from early September well into November. Through many crosses and hybridizations, chrysanthemums have been bred into shapes described as pompon, button, decorative, single, spoon, quill, anemone, spider, cascade, and exhibition. The flowers come in every color but blue. All need yearly division to look their best.

Eupatorium coelestinum

Hardy ageratum grows 18 to 36 inches tall, likes partial shade to full sun, does best in Zone 6, and flowers from August to mid-September. Pretty, upright stems carry fuzzy umbels of striking blue-violet florets, resembling the annual ageratum.

Helenium autumnale

Sneezeweed grows 2 to 4 feet tall, likes full sun, does best in Zone 3, and flowers from August to October. Bright yellow daisies with raised centers on tall stems bloom prolifically for many weeks in the fall. Named cultivars occur in shades of gold, orange, mahogany, reddish brown, and coppery orange.

Many lilies bring strong form and color into the late garden. Lily catalogs and suppliers will specify which of the hundreds of kinds will bloom until October.

Kirengeshoma palmata

Waxbells grow 3 to 4 feet tall, like partial shade, do best in Zone 5, and flower during September and October. This is a beautiful and useful late bloomer with large, maplelike leaves on arching, purplish-mauve stems. Sprays of pale yellow, waxy bells that resemble badminton shuttlecocks appear at the stem ends and from leaf axils.

Lilium hybrids and species

Lilies grow 2 to 8 feet tall, like full sun, do best in Zone 4, and flower from early August to October, depending on variety. Although many lilies bloom in late summer, others blossom until October, especially Division 7 Oriental hybrids, *Lilium henryi,* and *Lilium speciosum.* Colors include white, pink, crimson, salmon, orange, red, and gold. Flower shapes range from flat-faced to recurved, from trumpets to bowls.

Liriope muscari

Big blue lilyturf grows 12 to 18 inches tall, likes partial shade, does best in Zone 6, and flowers from mid-August to mid-September. Deep green, grassy, straplike leaves make a fine ground cover, from which spikes of grape–hyacinthlike flowers appear to give a color accent late in the year. The color is darker blue-violet than the bulb, and the flower spikes are much larger.

Salvia azurea

Blue sage grows 2 to 5 feet tall, likes full sun, does best in Zone 5, and flowers from late August until well into October. The true species has narrow leaves and terminal spikes of floppy, true blue flowers. The variety known as grandiflora is also sometimes sold as *Salvia pitcheri* and has larger, darker blue flower spikes. All need staking to prevent the flower spires from toppling over.

Sedum sieboldii

October Daphne grows 6 to 9 inches tall, likes full sun, does best in Zone 5, and flowers from late August until October. A trailing succulent with blue-green leaves and small clusters of tiny pink flowers, this is a good choice for a container and for a low ground cover in a well-tended spot.

Sedum spectabile 'Autumn Joy'

Showy stonecrop grows 1 to 2 feet tall, likes sun or light shade, does best in Zone 4, and flowers from late August until October. This interesting succulent with thick, lobed, pale green leaves produces a green, tightly packed flower head in August. It slowly turns pale pink, then darker pink, before ending its growing season in October with a reddish-mahogany color.

The succulent Sedum 'Autumn Joy,' in the foreground, has flower heads that begin as medium green, change to bright raspberry pink, deepen to burgundy, and finish as reddish brown.

THE
NATURAL
GARDEN

No straight-edged beds and borders here. This garden resembles a boggy spot where the rocks and water join the shade-loving plants to create a place of refreshment.

Landscaping is moving away from formal gardens and from the English style of beds and borders developed a century ago to a relaxed alternative. Many gardeners are now landscaping their properties in more natural ways. Such gardens take several forms.

The first might be called a naturalistic garden. The gardener brings the natural flora and appearance of the surrounding countryside onto the home property. Even a suburban or city lot can be planted to resemble the fields and woodlands that grew there before the land was developed.

Another form might be called the natural-site garden, created by using native plants in more planned ways—in beds and borders and in conditions that mimic nature, such as in a bog or on a sunny, dry slope.

Finally, a natural garden may take its design from nature, although not necessarily from something local. It might reproduce an Appalachian rock outcropping dressed with ferns, grasses, and shrubs in an Iowa field, or manzanita and oaks displayed on a California hillside.

THE NATURALISTIC GARDEN

To create a naturalistic garden on your property, you need to study an area where nature remains undisturbed by civilization.

National and state parks often are good places to look. So are areas with large trees that have not been logged for many years. Search for a natural area that is similar in soil

type and moisture availability to your property. It is pointless, for example, to assess plants in a wet area if your property lacks water.

OBSERVE AND MAKE NOTES

Take a notebook and several plant identification books so you can record the names of the trees, shrubs, and herbaceous plants you encounter. In the Northeast, for example, the original climax ecology was centered on a mixed hardwood forest. Look at the largest trees that form the forest canopy. You may find oak, hickory, beech, hornbeam, ash, maple, and birch, and other hardwoods. You'll also discover evergreens like hemlock, and softwood trees like the tulip tree, basswood, and aspen. Note their genus and species, the conditions where they

An open field has been densely planted with native birches to create a visual screen and tie the landscape to the surrounding woodlands.

173

*A **wildflower meadow of native herbaceous plants replaces a high-maintenance lawn, creating a colorful restoration of the native plant ecology.***

cohosh, stinging nettle, Virginia creeper, mayapple, trout lily, violet, and trillium.

Note as many as possible and indicate those you don't like and those that please you. For example, you may encounter greenbriar, poison ivy, and stinging nettles in the woods. You wouldn't want to plant these in your naturalistic garden. However, Solomon's-seal is beautiful, as are black cohosh, dogwoods, and Virginia creeper. Base your garden on your favorites, but don't ignore less attractive options; plants that associate in the wild want to be together in your garden.

Although this example assumes an eastern mixed hardwood forest, the rules of note-taking apply anywhere in the country, from the grassy prairies to the deserts of the Southwest, from the piney woods of the southeastern shore to the oak and manzanita chaparral of California.

grow (north, south, east, or west side of a hill; lowland; rocky slope; and so on), and how far apart they are. It will help to make a simple map showing the placement of trees in an area, perhaps 100 square feet, as a representation of climax woodland.

Under the canopy trees, you'll find slender, understory deciduous trees; large shrubs such as dogwood, redbud, spicebush, and witch hazel; and evergreen shrubs such as holly, rhododendron, and mountain laurel. A wide range of mostly herbaceous plants will grow near the ground. Some include black

PEST AND DISEASE RESISTANCE

Planting native vegetation is beneficial because it resists most of the pests and diseases native to the region and is perfectly adapted to the vagaries of soil and climate. Consequently, native plants are much easier to establish and maintain in good health than plants from widely different parts of the world.

WHERE SHOULD THE GARDEN GROW

Once you're home with your notebooks and maps, evaluate your property and consider its eventual use. The naturalistic garden will re-create the natural ecology of your region. It will be a place to visit, not a spot for football or outdoor parties. Place it on the margins of your property and consider paths through it, so visitors don't trample the native plants. The garden can be any size that supports a representative sample of natives or plants that have been wild so long that they act like natives.

If some of your property is already populated by native plants, the task will be simpler. Remove rank, diseased, and weedy plants, and leave healthy ones, adding as necessary to re-create the ecology of your region. If your property is adjacent to a natural area, extend the look of that area into your property with the same kinds of plants.

PLANTING SCHEME

Use your map and notes to plant the major canopy trees first, but don't place them as close together as they are in the wild. You aren't striving to imitate nature to the extent of creating a jumble of fallen trees and an impenetrable thicket of vines.

Place the canopy trees about one-third farther apart than they grow in the woods. Each tree will have more growing room and more exposure to sunlight, so it stays healthy. This spacing still allows a shady canopy to form.

Some azaleas are native North American woodland plants that have been selected and cultivated for bright displays of color; others come from Asia, making for a complex parentage.

Here the gardener has bordered a natural stream with tiered red primroses and Phlox divaricata, *giving a natural look but using only purchased plants.*

sunlight reaches the forest floor and sun-loving weeds and thorny plants will thrive. Control weed growth with thick mulches. They prevent weeds, keep the soil moist, and release nutrients.

If your naturalistic garden is out of sight of the house, you can let nature take its course and allow rough weeds to grow. Eventually, as the canopy closes, they will be replaced by native and well-adapted plants. It will just take longer and the mix will be selected by nature rather than by the gardener.

PLANTS FROM THE WILD

Never remove plants from the wild. Find them at a local native-plant nursery or at a nursery that grows them from seed or propagates them vegetatively. Always ask your plant supplier where the plants come from. Many native plants are "wildcrafted" (the euphemistic term for taking them from the wild). A better phrase for the practice would be "destruction of native plant communities." The most sought-after and beautiful plants are taken from the wild. This depletes natural areas of these favorites and may wipe them out in the wild. Moreover, the plants left behind are impoverished.

Position understory trees and shrubs farther apart as well, but plant thick drifts of herbaceous plants and wildflowers on the forest floor, where they look most natural. Large masses of the same plant scattered in drifts give a natural, parklike appearance.

CULTIVATE PATIENCE

Be prepared to wait. Saplings of native trees take from 10 to 20 years to grow large enough for the canopy to close. In the meantime,

The original North American tall-grass prairie was a wonderland of grasses and flowering plants, such as the drooping pink petals of Echinacea pallida and the yellow Rudbeckia hirta.

177

Prairie coneflower (Ratibida pinnata) *saturates this field with its small yellow petals.* In the background, *Prickly pear* (Opuntia Humifusa) pokes its head above the sea of yellow.

Many of the plants native to your area have been bred and crossed to produce superior cultivated varieties. Some of these hybrids and cultivars are as adaptive and easy to grow as the wild species; others may take more care. The cultivated varieties, however, have advantages.

The wild hickory, for instance, usually produces nuts so tough and small that it takes hours of painstaking work to produce a cupful of their incomparable nutmeats. Varieties of hickory have been bred in which the nuts are large and thin-shelled. You can crack out whole halves, as you can with the cultivated pecan, making shelling them much easier.

Similarly, the wild wood aster is small and dull, but cultivated varieties come in wide ranges of color and are as comfortable in their native range as the wood aster. The wild rosebay rhododendron has pretty pink to white flowers, but cultivated varieties come in many spectacular colors.

Asters grow wild by the roadsides
throughout much of the United States, so
the gardener here has sown large and
richly colored cultivated asters to brighten
an out-of-the-way part of the landscape.

As wild azaleas set color
throughout the woodlands, a
delicate lavender azalea sets
the color scheme in this inviting
backyard landscape.

Joe-Pye weed, cattails, and black-eyed Susans populate this cultivated but naturalistic landscape.

THE NATURAL-SITE GARDEN

Rather than inviting the surrounding ecology onto your property, the natural-site garden re-creates site-specific combinations of plants that may not have lived there before. A classic example is a bog garden. Such a garden can be created by hollowing out an area in which rainwater collects or in which water is supplied by irrigation.

Trees and woody plants that like bogs include the white pine and eastern larch, pin oak, willows, red maple, box elder, yellow birch, fringe tree, spicebush, wax myrtle, cranberries, and blueberries.

Some of the most beautiful bog-loving wildflowers are Joe-Pye weed, marsh mallow, violets, sundews, pitcher plants, watercress, star flower, queen of the prairie, marsh cinquefoil, purple avens, lysimachia, orange milkwort, pink field milkwort, forget-me-not, mints, mimulus, butterwort, twinflower, wapato, hatpins, rushes, cattails, arums, golden club, the endangered swamp pink, nodding trillium,

Establishing a naturalistic garden also will create a habitat for natural fauna. Birds, small mammals, insects, and other creatures that form the animal part of the native ecology will find your naturalistic garden inviting.

fairy wand, yellow flag, lady's slippers, calypso, rose pogonia, the fringed orchids, and grass pinks.

Lythrum salicaria is a good-looking bog plant so invasive that it is colonizing wetlands across the Northeast, forcing local governments to make it illegal. Avoid this plant.

GOOD GARDEN SITES

Other garden sites worthy of reproduction include a rocky woodland ledge, a meadow garden filled with prairie grasses and wildflowers, and a woodland garden filled with shade lovers. These kinds of gardens fit nicely into small, discrete areas prepared for them. Edge your garden with lawn, making it as approachable as any perennial bed.

A meadow of prairie grasses and wildflowers within view from a kitchen window is a superb idea. It doesn't have to be large to provide a pleasant view. You need to mow only once a year—usually in the fall after the grasses and wildflowers have ripened their seed—to keep the woody plants down.

A shady area created by mature pink dogwoods is the perfect setting for drifts of foamflowers, ferns, Solomon's-seal, and other woodland favorites. A slender path weaves its way back through the landscape's many delights.

Sedum 'Autumn Joy' and dried orna-mental grasses keep things natural looking and interesting among the ruins of this late-October garden in the Northeast.

large roots that turn up. Moisten the ground and cover it with clear plastic, burying the edges of the plastic. Solarize the soil for a few weeks in late May to kill weed seeds in the top 2 inches of soil. Remove the plastic and sow wildflower seeds without disturbing the soil more than necessary. Don't turn the soil any deeper than 2 inches or you'll turn up live weed seeds.

Plant native prairie grasses and any herbaceous plants you started as seedlings. Again, be careful not to spread the soil from the planting holes onto the surface. Keep the area well watered. Once the plants are established, remove any weeds and apply mulch. Keep after the weeds and perennial weedy grasses. Within two years your meadow will be a delightful combination of grasses and colorful wildflowers.

Try for a ratio of two or three grass plants to each wildflower specimen, spaced evenly over the plot. Grasses such as clumping carex, blue grama, sideoats grama, and bluestem are ideal. The wildflower mix should be suitable for full sun. Select either a prairie mix or one native to your region.

STARTING A MEADOW GARDEN

A meadow garden should be prepared in the spring. Select a full-sun area, dig up or rototill the site, and remove sod or turf. Remove

NATURAL LANDSCAPE DESIGN

You can create a third type of natural garden by reproducing a favored natural scene, even if it's not from your area. If you like the tall grasses that edge a watercourse, re-create the effect using a river of stones edged by giant

The joints between stones are choice areas for planting. Here lavender phlox flows down to meet white phlox at the base of these large rocks.

miscanthus. Or you may see wild shrubs growing in and around a naturally occurring group of large rocks. Reproduce the effect by bringing in rocks, arranging them as you saw them in nature, and planting shrubs to give a similar effect. It helps to photograph the original scene. As you travel on vacation, keep a camera ready to record scenes that appeal to you and can be reproduced at home. Even those far from home can be reproduced by substituting native or well-adapted plants for those you appreciated.

Echinacea purpurea, looks pretty in the informal setting of a wildflower meadow, and in the more formal garden, where it associates well with the yellows of Achillea taygetea 'Moonshine.'

183

AN EDIBLE
LANDSCAPE

Well-designed gardens appeal to all of our senses, including taste. Edible gardens allow you the pleasure of savoring a tree-ripened peach still warm from the sun or the luscious flavor of a vine-ripened tomato.

Too often the food garden is relegated to a utilitarian plot of straight rows and raised beds, planted for production and not for visual appeal. Why not plant edibles in a beautiful landscape?

Finding good things to eat as you explore the landscape makes gardening more fun, especially for children, who delight in encountering bushes full of berries and carrots ready to pull, wash, and eat. It may be difficult to get children to eat vegetables on a dinner plate, but they seldom need encouragement when they find something scrumptious in the garden.

DESIGN STRATEGIES

There are two strategies for creating landscapes with both food and flowers. One is to work edibles into the overall landscaping design. The other is to work flowering or aesthetically pleasing plants into the food garden. Both strategies can work on the same

Instead of just another shrub in a mixed ornamental border, put in a few blueberry bushes for their pretty berries, good fall color, and sweet taste they'll provide as you pass by.

property. For example, the main strawberry bed in the food garden also can be the nursery bed for strawberry plants you'll transplant elsewhere on the property.

When strawberries send out runners, you'll notice tufts of leaves at the nodes. Make sure these tufts touch the soil. If you keep the soil moist, they will soon put down roots. When the new plants have rooted, cut the long shoot that attaches them to the mother plant; dig up the new plant, being careful to preserve the root ball; and transplant it.

Strawberries make wonderful full-sun ground covers and companions for flowering plants in beds and borders, and under trees and shrubs where there's not too much shade. They're good in containers, on sunny hillsides, and anywhere the sun shines, the soil is good, and the moisture is plentiful.

The offspring of everbearing strawberries from your main strawberry beds will provide choice fruits everywhere you walk and garden, all summer long. The tiny alpine *Frais des Bois* are especially fragrant, flavorful, and beautiful.

VERSATILE GRAPES

Don't confine grapes to the garden trellis. They can provide shade for the back-yard arbor where summer dining occurs. In the fall, when the grapes are ripe, dessert hangs above the table.

Every farmhouse in France has a grapevine trained over the door. Pretty in all seasons,

Hide strawberries throughout your ornamental plantings.

Gooseberries are ornamental when their shrubby limbs are decked with flowers, and especially as their little round fruits ripen.

the vine is exceptionally attractive when it's in fruit and the leaves are turning red, yellow, burgundy, and orange. You also can train grapes along a fence that borders a walkway so visitors and family members can pick fruit as they use the walk.

In France and in California's wine country, shrub roses often flank the vine rows because they act as an early-warning system for mildew, which attacks the roses before it strikes grapes. When the vignerons see mildew on the roses, they know it's time to spray the grapes with a Bordeaux mixture—a relatively nontoxic fungicide. Besides the

practical aspects of combining these two plants, they are beautiful together.

BORDERS OF BERRIES

In mixed shrub borders, who says all the shrubs must be ornamentals? Add blueberries, huckleberries, black and red currants, gooseberries, and bush cherries here and there. A red currant bush loaded with strings of rich red berries makes a pretty picture in the July garden. Just plant them close to paths and walks so you can get to them; otherwise your shrub borders become dangerous as you try to reach the fruit.

Bramblefruits such as raspberries and blackberries can be invasive. Wise gardeners isolate them in beds with strong barriers at the edges so they can't send out stolons (underground running roots) to colonize the nearby turf.

Surround the bramble patch with a solid, nonrotting barrier such as sturdy plastic. Dig the plastic at least 2 feet into the soil. The underground runners will dive under barriers shallower than that.

Don't introduce bramblefruits to your ornamental plantings. Within a few years, they become impenetrable thickets that kill the ornamentals.

That doesn't mean that a patch of succulent red raspberries or wineberries arching into a path to offer fruit to passersby isn't a good idea. It's wonderful.

THORNY HEDGES

Blackberries have wicked thorns that point inward. You can insert an arm to gather berries, but the thorns will cut your arm when you withdraw it. Gooseberries have thorns that produce a quick, stabbing pain followed by a deep, focused ache. Some roses

Blackberries tend to volunteer in unkempt spots, but they are usually the very thorny wild types. Beat the wildings to the punch by putting in some thornless varieties with extra-large fruits.

are so thorny that their dried, dead canes are tied around bird-feeder poles to keep squirrels from climbing them. These three plants make great partners for a hedge that only the foolhardy will try to cross, but they also offer sweetness, beauty, and fragrance.

A good plant for both hedging and food production is the filbert. Plant filberts 4 feet apart in a row. Their roots send up many suckers, which finally grow together and form an impenetrable hedge that's 10 to 15 feet tall. With a mix of pollinators and several high-yield varieties like 'Ennis,' 'Butler,' and 'Barcelona,' the filbert hedge makes a good windbreak in summer; acts as a snow fence in winter; serves as a barrier to kids, dogs, and intruders; and showers you with a crop of delicious hazelnuts each fall, if you can beat the squirrels to them.

Dwarf apple trees produce more pounds of fruit per square foot of orchard space than larger trees, are easier to manage, and make a pretty landscape feature when they mature.

DWARF FRUIT TREES

Probably the least used and most productive plants for the home landscape are dwarf fruit trees. Dwarfing rootstocks are available that produce trees just 4 to 6 feet tall. Better for the landscape are the 9- to 13-foot-tall trees produced on the Mark or EMLA 26 dwarfing rootstocks. Small enough to be planted densely, dwarf fruit trees form miniature forests loaded with fruit.

Aisles and walks can wind among them, and they can be interplanted with shrubs, roses, herbs, and food crops in raised beds. The lower branches of dwarf trees can be trimmed so the trees provide a canopy of fruit. They are a perfect companion for steps, offering fruit to those walking up or down. Moreover, even their tallest branches can be reached easily for harvesting.

Dwarf fruit trees may become the trellis for a lovely clematis vine or for other vines that grow 6 to 10 feet tall. Select vines that won't smother the tree. Plant the area under the dripline with partial-shade flowers such as violas, impatiens, and petunias, or with foliage plants such as hostas. Or underplant with umbelliferous herbs, such as dill or fennel. They'll attract beneficial insects that reduce pests in the trees.

Espaliered fruit trees, like these apples trained along two wires, are pleasing landscape features, can edge a path, and produce delicious fruit.

ESPALIERED FRUIT TREES

Dress up drab fences with espaliered dwarf fruit trees. Space the trees about 8 feet apart along a fence, with one set of limbs extending upward to the left and another set extending upward to the right. The limbs from adjoining trees will cross at the tips.

Thin the fruit, especially apples, so there is no more than one fruit per foot of branch. Each tree will produce large, dessert-quality fruits in a compact, two-dimensional plane along the fence.

Training fruit trees into odd, unique, or eccentric shapes, like this pear espaliered against a wall, adds a vivacious touch to an otherwise plain-looking part of the property.

AN EDIBLE LANDSCAPE

Ornamental peppers and colored kales often are seen in late fall and early winter gardens in warmer climates, but they can brighten any garden if planted to ripen before frost.

Espaliers beautify plain walls with interesting plant designs and provide fruit. Choose semidwarf apples or pears. Erect a trellis 6 to 8 inches from the wall. Walls facing east, south, or west will support a crop of fruit, but a shady north wall will not.

VINING CROPS

Do you have a sunny bank that's hard to mow? Consider planting annual, food-producing, vining plants such as melons, cucumbers, and squashes to trail down the bank. Dig large holes 6 feet apart at the top of the bank and fill them with rich compost, then plant. If you're growing watermelons or pumpkins, support the fruits so they don't roll down the hill and pull the vines with them. Drive stakes into the bank below them when they are small or sling them in an onion bag pinned to the bank with a stake. Vining plants like sun and will smother weeds with their thick growth.

Surmount a small hill or berm with bush squashes. One green zucchini and one yellow squash plant provide a family with a summer's supply of squash. Their big yellow blossoms and pretty squashes are ornamental as well.

DECORATIVE VEGETABLES

Garden vegetables such as eggplant and okra have flowers and fruit pretty enough to be featured in an ornamental garden. Eggplant

has interesting flowers and fruit, especially the small, oblong or egg-shaped, white Japanese varieties. The bright colors of ripe peppers also add splashes of red and yellow.

Scarlet runner beans have bright red flowers that are decorative on fences and trellises. They bring the added benefit of green beans for the pot and dry shell beans if you let them dry on the vine.

Many herbs are pretty and attract bees that pollinate other flowers. Borage, for example, has myriad clear, blue flowers that taste like cucumber, brighten any garden, and can be used to decorate cakes,

The snappy red flowers of the scarlet runner bean are visually strong enough to be part of the ornamental landscape, but also are a wonderful decoration for summer salads.

cold drinks, and salads. Thyme makes a fine edging for an ornamental garden.

Red leaf lettuces provide interesting foliage color and fluffy leaf texture planted beneath ornamental shrubs. In midsummer, lettuces and salad greens will appreciate the shade thrown by ornamentals overhead.

PROPAGATING GREATNESS

Although fruits and vegetables can enliven ornamental gardens, the reverse also is true. Often productive vegetable gardens are devoid of flowers. One strategy is to allow the best-looking plant or two in a vegetable row to grow after you've pulled the others. You can replant the bed with an ornamental crop, but the last two vegetable specimens will flower

This border features an exquisite mixture of edibles and ornamentals, including rosemary, chives, dianthus, hollyhocks, cardoon, and angelica.

Lettuce varieties love a little cool company during summer's heat. Here ruffle-edged greens are tucked among dianthus, violas, alyssum, and daisies.

197

mightily and produce seed, which you can save. Repeat this process with open-pollinated varieties, and you become a gardener who perpetuates greatness in vegetables by reproducing only the best. Besides, a new bed looks more friendly and useful when the baby plants are sheltered by a mature plant or two towering above them in full bloom.

MASSED PLANTINGS

Remember that plant-destroying insects are more apt to find their favorite plants when they are massed in the garden. Mix vegetable plants with those that insects rarely touch: mints, artemisias, and annual and perennial flowers such as marigolds, rudbeckia, and helenium. The only garden crops that should be planted en masse are those that require lots of pollen in the air to set their crops. Sweet corn is an example.

Mounds of cabbages and other crucifers yield a heavy crop among a sea of bright marigolds for a stunning edible landscape effect.

Seed-bearing sunflowers with giant heads and the many ornamental sunflowers, such as the Inca strains, decorate the garden beautifully. Plant them behind tall corn or trellised plants so their heads hang over the top.

Alternate rows of crops and flowers in the garden, so a row of vegetables is bordered on each side by everlastings for dried arrangements or sun-loving perennials for fresh-cut flowers. This kind of staggered planting also disrupts the ability of insects to find host plants.

The range of edible, decorative flowers is large. The florets of garlic chives and onions are tasty, as are calendula petals, borage, the light lavender florets of mint, and oregano and thyme.

Not every edible flower is palatable, however, and some are best reserved for decoration. Violas, including Johnny-jump-ups, fall into that category. So do impatiens and tulbaghia (society garlic), with its overbearing garlicky smell and flavor.

Keep an eye open for edible plants you think would be attractive in landscaping and for ornamentals that would dress up the food garden. Break the boundaries of the food and flower gardens, mixing the two in an edible landscape that offers visual appeal and good taste to those who visit or garden there.

PART THREE:
OUTDOOR PROJECTS

TIMBER AND BRICK STEPS

Wood and bricks make a warm and welcoming stairway that requires no special equipment beyond a few basic landscaping and carpentry tools. An impressive improvement on crumbling concrete, these stairs are as suitable for formal entryways as they are for steps up to an informal patio area. Within a couple of weekends you can be accenting these steps with colorful plantings.

GETTING READY

- 6x6 timbers are a good choice: Their 5½-inch dimension makes for an easy riser height. (Keep the treads 11½ inches deep for a comfortable single pace between stairs.) If you use larger landscaping timbers, be sure they are not too rough for foot traffic. Pave the steps with SW (severe weather) brick (common brick probably will not be strong enough), or use concrete pavers.
- Rent an oversize circular saw or chain saw to cut the timbers. In addition to basic carpentry and excavation tools, you'll need a ⅜-inch extension drill bit, mallet, baby sledge, brickset, line level, mason's line, and hand tamper. This invloves some fairly heavy work, enlist help.

MATERIALS LIST
- ☐ SW (severe weather) brick, or bricklike concrete pavers
- ☐ 6x6 or 6x8 timbers
- ☐ gravel
- ☐ precut 2' pieces of ⅜" reinforcing bar (available from landscape material suppliers)
- ☐ 12" galvanized spikes
- ☐ weed barrier: PVC sheeting or weed block fabric
- ☐ coarse sand base
- ☐ fine sand for filling between bricks

1 The rise of each step is established by the thickness of the timber. The total distance your stairs climb most likely will not be evenly divisible by that thickness. Make up the difference at the lowest step and beneath the door sill. Mark a 1x2 to make a story pole and, with a line level and mason's line, determine your layout. (A straight 2x4 and a carpenter's level can be used if the distance is short enough.)

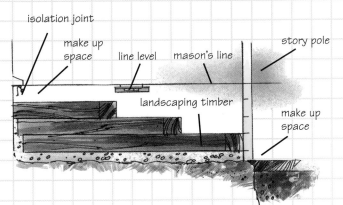

isolation joint

make up space

line level

mason's line

story pole

landscaping timber

make up space

2 Excavate the site, allowing 6 inches of working space on each side. Lay a 2-inch bed of gravel base for the bottom timbers. Use a level to make sure the steps slope away from the house ⅛ inch per foot. For timbers whose tops will not show, pound 2-foot precut sections of reinforcing bar down through ⅜-inch holes every 3 feet or so. For other timbers, use 12-inch spikes.

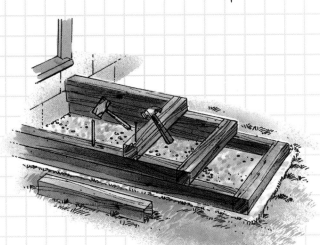

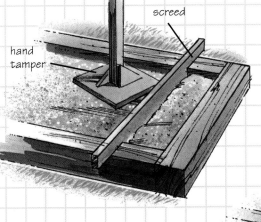

screed

hand tamper

3 For each step, tamp the soil firm, line with weed barrier, and fill with 2 to 3 inches of coarse sand. Screed the sand so it is smooth and allows space for bricks or pavers to sit on top. Tamp the sand smooth and firm.

whisk broom

tamped sand

4 Install bricks or pavers, cutting them with a baby sledge and brickset when necessary (see Brick Raised Bed, page 274). Pour fine sand on the paved surface and brush until the cracks are filled. Hose it down, brush in more sand, and hose it down again. Repeat as necessary.

rubber mallet

203

CONCRETE STEPS

Concrete steps are solid, reliable, and relatively inexpensive to build. After excavation, steps can be formed and poured in two days. However, installing them is not a casual affair: Any mistakes will, as they say, be set in concrete. Finishing is the most difficult step. If you do not have experience smoothing concrete, ask someone who does to help.

GETTING READY

- If you are removing an existing set of steps, take note of their dimensions—especially the rise and run of the steps. If you plan to install an outward-swinging storm door, add 20 inches depth to the landing.
- In addition to basic carpentry tools, you'll need a post-hole digger and concrete finishing tools.
- With plastic sheeting, cover any surfaces of the house that could get spattered.
- Choose the type of railing you will use. Some require fitting preparation as the concrete is formed; others are attached after the concrete is set.
- If you cannot arrange to have the concrete truck pour directly into the form, use a wheelbarrow and a plank or plywood runway for wheeling the concrete to the site.

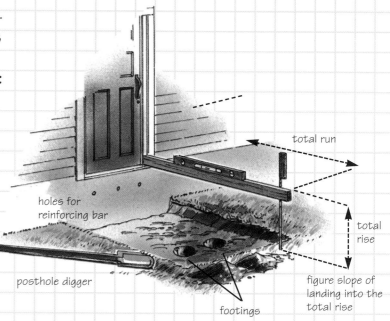

total run

total rise

holes for reinforcing bar

posthole digger

footings

figure slope of landing into the total rise

MATERIALS LIST

- ☐ 4x8x¾" plywood for forms
- ☐ 2x4s for stakes and braces
- ☐ 2x8s for front of forms
- ☐ 2 pounds 16d double–headed (duplex head) nails
- ☐ 2 pounds 7d common nails
- ☐ isolation joint material to cover the entire area where the stairway meets the house
- ☐ (3) precut reinforcing bars, 2' long
- ☐ car oil and an old paintbrush

1 Excavate the site, allowing an extra 6 inches on each side. At the base of the stairway, dig two footings that extend below the frost line. The steps must be uniform in height (rise) and depth (run). (See Geometric Deck, page 245.) To measure the total rise, use a straight 2x4 and a carpenter's level.

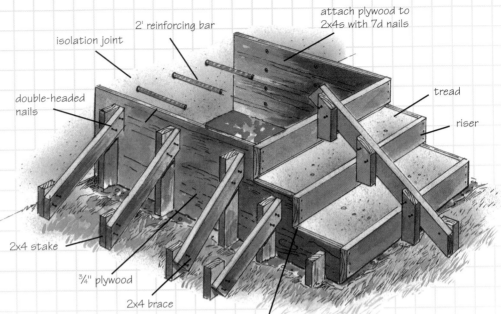

2 Drill holes and insert reinforcing bar at least 3 inches into the foundation. Install a sheet of isolation joint. Build the form as shown: Bevel the 2x8s at the bottom and rip them to height. Make sure the steps will be pitched forward ⅛ inch per foot so water will run off.

isolation joint

2' reinforcing bar

attach plywood to 2x4s with 7d nails

tread

riser

double-headed nails

2x4 stake

¾" plywood

2x4 brace

bottom edge of 2x8 riser form is beveled at 15°

apply oil with an old paintbrush

3 Stack rubble (concrete chunks, stone, brick) in the form, taking care that none of the fill comes closer than 4 inches to the form or the finished concrete surface. Brush oil on the inside of the form. Pour the concrete, starting at the bottom tread. Let it stiffen before continuing to pour. Tamp the concrete with a piece of board as you go, then screed the surface. Gently tap the forms to eliminate air pockets. Once the steps have set sufficiently to stand in place (this can take anywhere from 30 minutes to a few hours depending on the weather), remove the 2x8 riser forms.

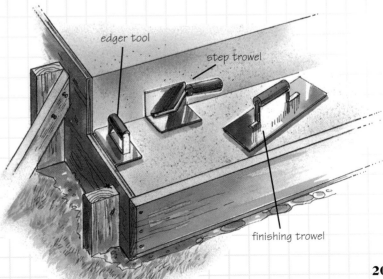

edger tool

step trowel

4 Finish the surface with a concrete finishing trowel, using light, circular motions to bring the moisture to the surface. Use a step trowel for the inside step corner and an edger tool for the outside corner edges. When the steps have cured, remove the forms. Cover any voids in the sides with concrete patching compound.

finishing trowel

205

BRICK PATH

Brick paths have an old-world charm that complements any landscaping style. With bricks you can create almost any shape of walkway you want, from a straight and narrow formal walk to a meandering path. In addition, the options in brick patterns offer design versatility. Bricks set in sand are less stable than those set in concrete, but the gentle undulations of a well-worn brick path are part of the charm of this traditional landscaping material.

GETTING READY

- Calculate the total area of the path. Tell your material supplier what patterns you'll use (see next page), so material can be estimated accurately.
- Plan on making the path at least 36 inches wide so two people can walk comfortably side by side.
- Lay out the path, using the hardboard form to shape the curves. (Position one form on one side of the walk only. The other form will be positioned once most of the brick is in place.)
- Gather together the special tools needed for this project: a carpenter's level, measuring tape, shovels, a rake for smoothing the sand, a hand tamper, goggles and gloves, a brickset, and a baby sledge.

MATERIALS LIST

- ☐ 4"-wide ¼" hardboard strips
- ☐ 2x2x12" stakes
- ☐ coarse sand
- ☐ SW (severe weather) bricks
- ☐ weed barrier: PVC sheeting or weed-block fabric
- ☐ 1" deck screws

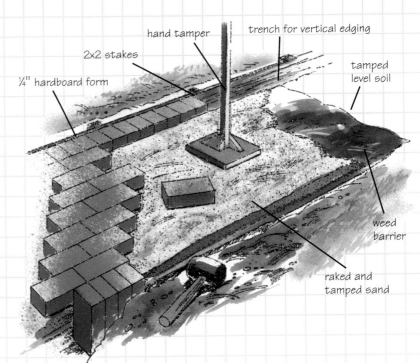

1 Excavate for the walkway by digging 5 inches down and at least 4 inches wider than the finished path. Edging with upright bricks requires a trench along each side of the path 1 inch deeper than the brick length. Pound in 2x2 stakes, level the hardboard, and fasten it to the stakes with 1-inch deck screws, adding wood shims where needed to even the hardboard form. Install the edging bricks along one side of the path (you will add the other side later). Use sand to bring them up to the desired level. When the edging is complete, smooth the bottom of the excavation and lay down weed barrier. Add enough sand so the bricks can be set even with the edging bricks. Rake and tamp the sand.

hand tamper
trench for vertical edging
2x2 stakes
¼" hardboard form
tamped level soil
weed barrier
raked and tamped sand

2 Using the edging bricks as a guide, level each brick by filling in with a splash of sand or tapping the brick with a rubber mallet. Lay the path with a slight crown in the center. Once you've completed the full width of the path, add the second edging. Finally, sweep sand between the brick and moisten. Fill, sweep, and moisten three times, then remove the forms and backfill along the walk.

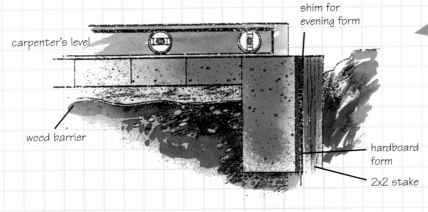

shim for evening form
carpenter's level
weed barrier
hardboard form
2x2 stake

PATTERN OPTIONS

Running

Stack Bond

Herringbone

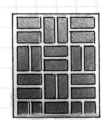
Basket Weave

Diagonal Herringbone

Double Basket Weave

Capped Herringbone

Running and Stack Bond Mixed

207

CONCRETE PAVER WALKWAY

Concrete pavers offer a wide range of colors and patterns, are easy to install, and are relatively inexpensive. They require only a firm, smooth base of sand and some sweat equity. Held in by sturdy edging, concrete pavers are easy to install and offer many of the virtues of concrete.

GETTING READY

• Establish the width of the path by laying out a row of pavers. Choose a layout that requires minimal cutting. Your path should be at least 3 feet wide.

• Keep the path at least 2 feet away from trees, large bushes, and hedges.

MATERIALS LIST

☐ redwood, cedar, or pressure-treated 2x4s
☐ 2x6 for screed
☐ stakes, 8d galvanized common nails
☐ weed barrier: PVC sheeting or weed-block fabric
☐ pavers and sand

1 After laying out your walkway, excavate to a depth of 6 inches. Install 2x4 edging, mitering joints and staking every 4 feet. Level across the walkway. Tamp the soil firm, removing any roots ½ inch or more in diameter. Add steps if the walkway must incline more than 10 percent.

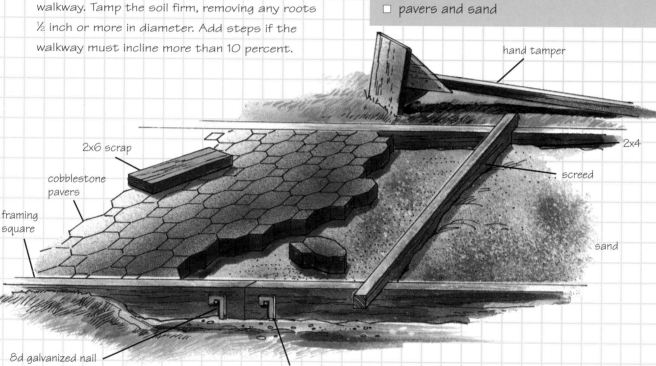

hand tamper

2x6 scrap

cobblestone pavers

framing square

2x4

screed

sand

8d galvanized nail

manufactured stake

2 Install the weed barrier. Make a screed from a 2x6, notching it equal to the thickness of the pavers. Add enough sand to form a 2-inch layer. Screed the sand to form a level bed. Moisten and tamp the sand until it is well packed and smooth.

3 Set the pavers in place. Cut the blocks by first scoring and then cutting them with a baby sledge and a brick-set (as shown on page 212). Use a framing square to true up the courses every few feet. Finally, spread sand on the walkway. Sweep away the excess and moisten. Repeat this process until the joints between the pavers are filled.

PLATFORM WALKWAY

Nothing tames damp or awkward terrain quite so well as a platform walkway. This affordable solution is constructed much like a simple deck: 4x4s sunk in postholes bear a 2x6 frame to which 2x6 decking is fastened. These platforms can be set to step down a difficult slope or inclined 1 foot in 12 feet for a comfortable descent.

GETTING READY

- Pressure-treated lumber is necessary for this ground-hugging structure.
- Plan on a walkway 36 inches wide with footings every 8 feet.
- Gather together the tools needed for this project: a posthole digger, shovel, rake, mason's line and stakes, and basic carpentry tools.

1 Begin by constructing the 2x6 frames. Use them as guides for digging all of the postholes. Install the posts along one side of the frame first. Pour 3 inches of gravel into each posthole, set and plumb the posts, and then pack gravel around them. Fasten one side of the frame to each post with lag bolts, leveling the frame as you go. Using the frame as a guide, install the opposite row of posts and fasten them to the frame. Trim tops of the 4x4 posts flush with the frame.

lag bolts

2x6

1½" space

2x6 frame

gravel

weed barrier

posthole

2 Lay down a weed barrier and pea gravel to inhibit plant growth beneath the walkway. Cut 2x6s to 36 inches and fasten them to the frame joists with 3-inch deck screws, maintaining a ¼-inch gap between treads. Square up the treads occasionally with a framing square.

MATERIALS LIST

- ☐ 4x4 posts
- ☐ 2x6 joists
- ☐ 2x6 decking
- ☐ 3" galvanized deck screws,
- ☐ ¼x6" hex-headed bolts, nuts, washers
- ☐ gravel
- ☐ weed barrier: PVC sheeting or weed-block fabric

209

CRUSHED STONE PATH

Crushed stone makes a handsome walkway that is easy on the feet. Relatively inexpensive and easy to install, this walkway blends into almost any landscape. The addition of flexible edging allows for gentle curves and keeps the material in place. With replenishing every few years, this path will serve for decades.

GETTING READY

- Use a garden hose to lay out the curving sides of your path. It can be as free-form as you like—these materials lend themselves to flexibility.

- Plan on making your path at least 36 inches wide so two people can walk comfortably side by side.

- Purchase precut, pressure-treated log sections. Determine the quantity needed by measuring the total linear feet of edging you'll require and dividing it by the diameter of a log section.

1 Excavate for the path at least 4 inches below grade. On each side of the path dig a 12-inch-deep trench for the log sections, making each trench at least 2 inches wider than the logs. Add 2 inches of gravel to the bottom of the trench to slow the deterioration of the wood. Tap the log sections in place with a mallet. The tops of the logs needn't be even, but the sides should be plumb. Use a level to check occasionally.

crushed stone

coarse sand

12" deep trench

6x24" log section

soil

weed barrier

MATERIALS LIST

- ☐ 6x24" log sections
- ☐ weed barrier: PVC sheeting or weed-block fabric
- ☐ coarse sand
- ☐ crushed stone
- ☐ gravel for setting log sections

2 Roll out the weed barrier and add a 1-inch layer of coarse sand, packing it around the log sections. Tamp the sand firmly. Add the stone, first raking it and then tamping it level. Backfill along the outside of the logs, first with sand, then with moistened topsoil.

LOOSE-FILL PATH

Loose organic materials such as bark nuggets, chipped wood, cypress mulch, and crushed seashells are among the least expensive options for paths. Protected from plant infiltration by a weed barrier and edged to keep the material from washing away, this walkway can last for many years.

MATERIALS LIST

- ☐ loose-fill organic material
- ☐ weed barrier: PVC sheeting or weed-block fabric
- ☐ edging material

GETTING READY

- Buying loose organic materials by the bag is far more expensive than purchasing in bulk. Typically sold by the square yard (27 cubic feet), a local landscaping firm, garden center, and even some municipalities, will deliver the desired quantity to your site.
- Lay out your walkway in advance. Loose-fill materials adjust readily to contours and configurations.
- A shovel, rake, and wheelbarrow are the main tools you'll need.

2 Edge the path to keep the material from being kicked out. Stones set on grade provide a pleasing contrast to the loose material. Plastic edging is even easier and less expensive. Distribute the path material liberally as it will quickly settle.

1 Dig the area to a depth of 4 inches below grade using a flat spade. Rake the area smooth and spread fabric weed barrier.

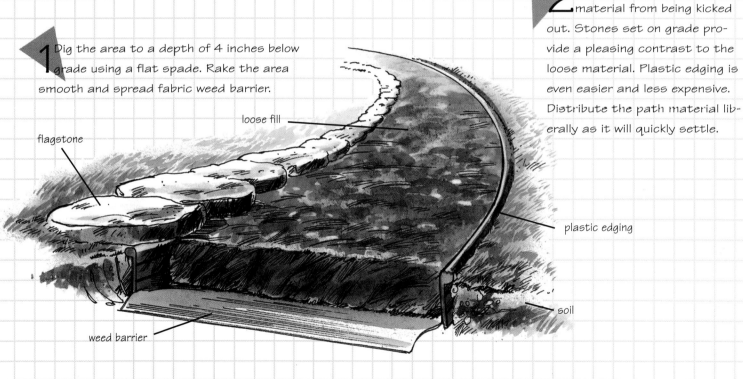

loose fill

flagstone

plastic edging

soil

weed barrier

Pine Bark Nuggets

Chipped Wood

Cypress Mulch

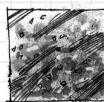

Crushed Seashells

FLAGSTONE PATH

Whether flagstone walkways grace informal or formal gardens, they always lend a sense of timeless beauty. Adjustable to any shape or configuration, stone takes the edge off overly geometric landscapes.

MATERIALS LIST

- ☐ coarse sand
- ☐ weed barrier: PVC sheeting or weed-block fabric
- ☐ flagstone
- ☐ limestone screenings

GETTING READY

- Stone is sold by the ton. A ton of 2-inch-thick flagstone will cover about 90 square feet. However, coverage varies according to thickness, so tell your stone supplier the total square footage you wish to cover.
- Have the stone delivered as close to your work site as possible.
- Gather the special tools needed, including a baby sledge, brickset, and hand tamper.
- Use gloves and eye protection when cutting stone.

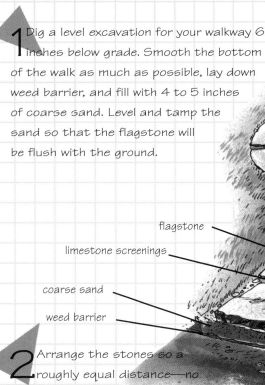

1 Dig a level excavation for your walkway 6 inches below grade. Smooth the bottom of the walk as much as possible, lay down weed barrier, and fill with 4 to 5 inches of coarse sand. Level and tamp the sand so that the flagstone will be flush with the ground.

flagstone

limestone screenings

coarse sand

weed barrier

2 Arrange the stones so a roughly equal distance—no more than 1 inch—is between them on all sides. This is the art in laying stone. Take time to arrange the best possible combination. Finally, force the stones into the sand, maintaining a level surface.

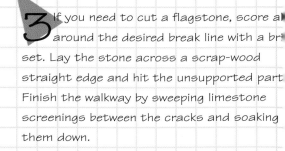

3 If you need to cut a flagstone, score all around the desired break line with a brickset. Lay the stone across a scrap-wood straight edge and hit the unsupported part. Finish the walkway by sweeping limestone screenings between the cracks and soaking them down.

Rather than spending thousands of dollars to tear out a concrete slab and refill it with topsoil, consider building a trellislike pergola. This airy, yet sturdy, structure can be built in two or three weekends. Ideal for climbing plants, it creates an area of dappled sunlight that's delightful for entertaining. You can make it as shady as you like by adding climbing plants and creepers, or by topping off the structure with a sheet of fabric. The four corners of the pergola are anchored with planter boxes.

GETTING READY

- Use rot-resistant lumber, either pressure-treated or the heartwood of cedar or redwood.
- No special tools are required, but a hammer drill for boring into concrete and a power miter saw will make the job easier.
- Have two 12-foot stepladders on hand. While you are building, the structure will be unsteady, with nothing solid on which to lean an extension ladder.
- You'll need assistance in raising some of the members into place. Line up helpers in advance.

MATERIALS LIST (for 16'x20' structure)

- ☐ (8) 4"x4"x10' posts
- ☐ (2) 2"x6"x20', (4) 2"x6"x12', (3) 2"x6"x8' framing members
- ☐ (31) 2"x6"x16' rafters (spaced 8" apart)
- ☐ (12) 2"x4"x8' braces
- ☐ (32) 1"x4"x8' for planter boxes
- ☐ (2) 2"x2"x12' for planter-box frames
- ☐ (4) galvanized U-brackets for anchoring middle posts
- ☐ ¼x3" galvanized lag screws with shields
- ☐ 2 pounds 3" galvanized deck screws
- ☐ 2 pounds 1⅝" galvanized deck screws
- ☐ 1 pound 1" galvanized deck screws
- ☐ wood preservative
- ☐ hurricane ties
- ☐ galvanized 3-sided corner brackets

LANDSCAPING PROJECTS
PERGOLA

1 The pergola is constructed by first cutting and positioning the corner posts, then setting the overhead framing in place. Begin by trimming the corner posts to 10 feet. Soak the bottom 18 inches of each post in wood preservative. Set the posts in position and temporarily brace them. On paved areas, anchor the braces with concrete blocks; otherwise, stake them in place. Check that each post is plumb.

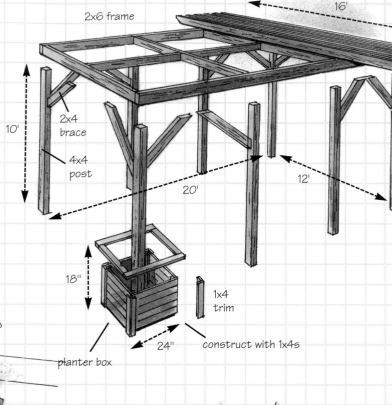

2x6 frame

16'

10'

2x4 brace

4x4 post

20'

12'

18"

1x4 trim

24'

construct with 1x4s

planter box

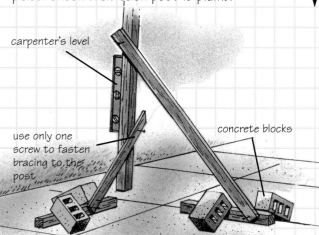

carpenter's level

use only one screw to fasten bracing to the post

concrete blocks

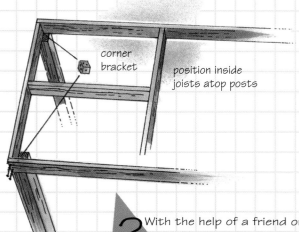

corner bracket

position inside joists atop posts

2 With the help of a friend or two, construct the top frame in place with 2x6s and 3-inch galvanized screws. Fasten the frame to the corner posts with angled 3-inch deck screws or three-sided corner brackets.

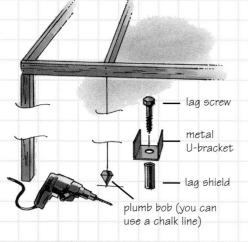

lag screw

metal U-bracket

lag shield

plumb bob (you can use a chalk line)

3 Mark the position of the remaining posts. Drill holes in the concrete for the shields and securely attach U-brackets with lag screws.

4 Trim each of the remaining posts to size. (Take into account how high the anchors will hold them off the slab. Also, the posts may differ in length due to variations in the slab.) Drill a hole in the bottom of each post to fit over the lag screw head. Set each in place, check for plumb, and attach to the frame with angle-driven screws or corner brackets.

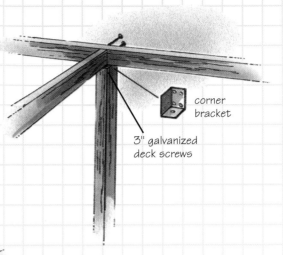

corner bracket

3" galvanized deck screws

5 On the overhead 2x6, mark the halfway point between each pair of posts along the sides (not the front) of the structure. Measure and mark the same distance down from the top of each post. Measure between the two marks to determine the length of the long side of each 2x4 angled brace. Cut both ends of each brace at a 45-degree angle and attach with 3-inch deck screws.

6 Cut 2x6 and use it as a template for the others. Experiment with different spacings: Closer together, they create more shade. Attach with hurricane ties and 1-inch screws.

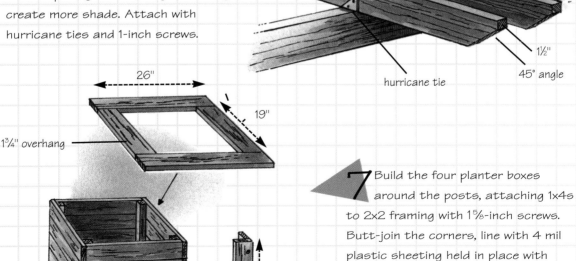

1½"

hurricane tie

45° angle

26"

19"

1¾" overhang

17¼"

24"

22½"

7 Build the four planter boxes around the posts, attaching 1x4s to 2x2 framing with 1⅝-inch screws. Butt-join the corners, line with 4 mil plastic sheeting held in place with staples, and cover with 1x4 trim pieces. Top it off with a 1x4 ledge and fill with soil.

ARCHED ARBOR

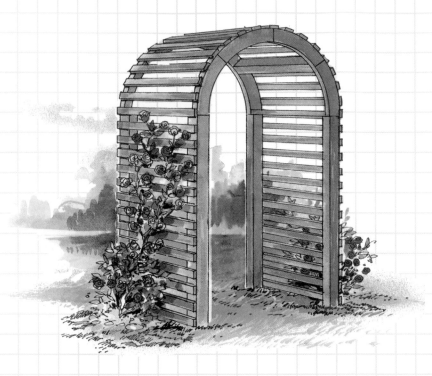

This sturdy arbor makes a romantic entryway or practical divider for your landscaping plan. Once climbing flowers are established, the arbor will be an eye-catching, softening feature. The overhead arch, cut from 2x8s, is easier to build than it might look. And with 4x4s as the primary framing members, the arbor has a substantial look.

GETTING READY

- Choose lumber that will stand up to your weather conditions. (Remember that if you are going to have plants climbing over the structure, they will tend to hold moisture on the arbor.) If you plan to treat or paint the arbor, consider doing so before you build—painting the crosspieces in place is difficult and time-consuming.
- In addition to basic carpentry tools, rent a heavy-duty saber saw for cutting the curved pieces.
- You will need to enlist a helper to assemble the arches.

MATERIALS LIST

- ☐ (4) 4"x 4"x 8' for posts
- ☐ (2) 2"x6"x8' for arches
- ☐ (1) 4"x4"x8' for arch braces
- ☐ (1) 2"x4"x6' for arch braces
- ☐ (11) 1"x3"x12' (if 1x3 is unavailable, substitute 1x2 or 1x4)
- ☐ 1 pound 3" galvanized deck screws
- ☐ (6) 3x¾-inch mending plates for temporarily holding arch pieces together
- ☐ 3 pounds 1⅝" galvanized deck screws
- ☐ 1 pound 1" screws for temporary bracing
- ☐ gravel for the postholes

1 On a large piece of cardboard, draw a template for your arches, using a compass made from a nail, a string, and a pencil. Using a framing square and protractor, divide the arch into four equal sections and cut out the four arches.

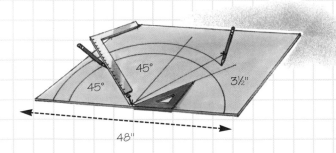

2 On the 2x8, use the cardboard pieces to mark for your arch members. Cut them out with a jig saw. Temporarily attach your arches together with 3x¾-inch mending plates. (You will remove them after the arbor is assembled.)

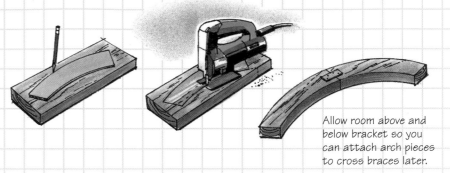

Allow room above and below bracket so you can attach arch pieces to cross braces later.

3 Dig the postholes below the frost line and shovel a little gravel into the bottom of each. Set the posts in and temporarily brace them into position, checking for plumb in all directions. Starting with one post, mark a point 7 feet above the ground. Level across to the other posts and mark them. Use a square to draw a line around each post, and cut it with a hand saw or circular saw.

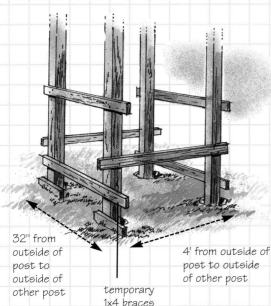

32" from outside of post to outside of other post

temporary 1x4 braces

4' from outside of post to outside of other post

4x4 brace

2x4 brace

predrill all screw holes

3" deck screws

4 Attach 2x4 horizontal braces to the top of the posts, leaving 1½ inches of space at each end for the arches. Position the arches, then attach the 4x4 horizontal braces, cut to the same length as the horizontal 2x4 braces. Install the crosspieces, using a scrap of 1x3 as a spacer. Once everything is in place, gradually fill the holes and tamp the posts in place.

217

SQUARE ARBOR

Here's a solid portal topped with a bit of elegant whimsy. Heavy 6x6 posts set in concrete provide firm support for the specially cut flying pieces on top, making a substantial entryway or focal point for your landscaping. While the most demanding task will be cutting the shaped ends of the "flying" joists, a person with average carpentry skills can produce this impressive garden feature. Allow a couple of weekends for the project.

GETTING READY

- Use rot-resistant wood for this project such as redwood, cedar, or pressure-treated lumber—there are plenty of places where moisture can settle. If you find that you cannot get 6x6s in your chosen material, use a protective stain to blend the pressure-treated lumber with cedar or redwood.
- Plan on digging the postholes and setting the posts on the first weekend, allowing five days for the concrete to set and cure.
- Paint or treat the pieces before you assemble them—perhaps while the concrete is curing.
- You will need a heavy-duty jig saw or band saw to cut the curved ends of the 2x6s.
- When cutting through the 6x6 posts, make the initial perpendicular cut with a circular saw, then finish with a handsaw.
- Have a sturdy stepladder on hand. Draft an assistant to help install the top pieces.

MATERIALS LIST

- ☐ (4) 6"x6"x12' for posts
- ☐ (9) 2"x6"x8' for "flying" rafters
- ☐ (7) 1"x2"x8' for top pieces
- ☐ (5) 1"x2"x8' for nailers and molding
- ☐ (2) 4'x8' prefab lattice panels
- ☐ (2) 2"x4"x8' for braces
- ☐ (1) 2"x10"x4' for post caps
- ☐ concrete and gravel for postholes
- ☐ 2 pounds 3" galvanized deck screws
- ☐ 1 pound 1⅝" galvanized deck screws
- ☐ 1 pound 1¼" galvanized deck screws
- ☐ 1 pound 6d galvanized finishing nails

1 Make a cardboard template for cutting the 2x6s. Draw a rectangle 5½ inches wide and at least 17 inches long to represent the 2x6. With a compass, draw arcs from the points shown. Cut the template out of the cardboard with a utility knife. Use a heavy-duty jig saw to make the cuts.

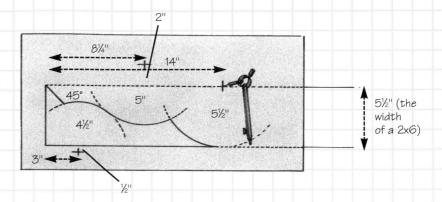

8¼" 2" 14"

45° 5"

4½" 5½"

3" ½"

5½" (the width of a 2x6)

2 Begin framing by digging postholes deeper than the frost line. Add 2 inches of gravel and set the posts. Connect the posts with temporary bracing, check for plumb in all directions, and pour the concrete. Allow five days for the concrete to set and cure.

3 Cut all the posts level with each other, about 9¼ feet above the ground. Attach the four lower flying pieces to the sides of the posts with 3-inch galvanized deck screws. Add 1x2 trim beneath each, using 6d finishing nails Either butt the ends as shown, or miter the corners.

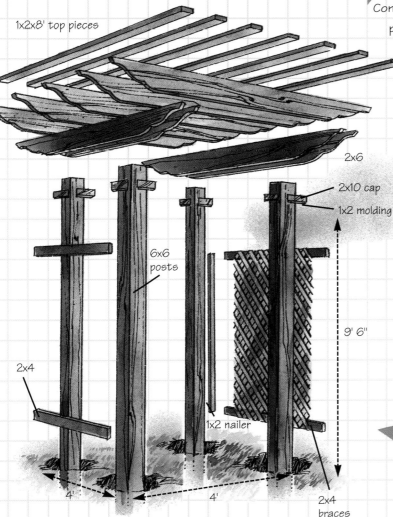

1x2x8' top pieces

2x6

2x10 cap

1x2 molding

6x6 posts

2x4

9' 6"

1x2 nailer

4'   4'

2x4 braces

4 Then lay out the upper pieces so they are evenly spaced, and attach by predrilling holes and driving 3-inch deck screws at an angle. Top the structure off with the 1x2 pieces, using 1⅝-inch screws.

5 Cut the lattice sheet so that it overhangs the braces evenly at the top and bottom, and attach it with 1¼-inch screws. On the inside of the arbor, attach the 1x2 nailers with 1⅝-inch screws, and screw the lattice into the nailers.

219

TRIANGULAR ARBOR

Of the three arbor projects in this book, this is the easiest to build. The clean, spare lines of this arbor will fit into any section of your yard. Once the posts have been set, the rest of the structure can be built in a half day. Widely spaced 1x3 braces allow room for robust plants to climb, but are far enough apart to discourage small children from using the trellis as a jungle gym.

GETTING READY

- Choose wood that will last in your climate. If you plan to paint the structure, pressure-treated lumber is an affordable choice.
- 1x3s are needed for side braces. If your lumberyard does not have 1x3s, they should be able to rip 1x6s to size for a modest cutting fee.
- In addition to basic carpentry tools, you will need a posthole-digger, a shovel, and something in which to mix concrete—a deep wheelbarrow or plastic mortar box. Rent a power miter saw if you are not confident about making accurate 45-degree cuts on the 2x4 rafters.
- With a posthole digger, excavate postholes that extend below the frost line or at least 24 inches deep. Pour in 2 to 3 inches of gravel. This keeps the bottom of your posts from direct contact with the soil.

MATERIALS LIST

- ☐ (4) 4"x4"x12' for posts (10-footers will work if your postholes are shallower than 24")
- ☐ (2) 2"x4"x8' for top plates
- ☐ (2) 2"x4"x12' for rafters
- ☐ (2) 1"x3"x14' for sidepieces
- ☐ (2) 1"x3"x10' for roof pieces
- ☐ 1 pound 3" galvanized deck screws
- ☐ 2 pounds 1⅝" galvanized deck screws
- ☐ concrete and gravel for the postholes
- ☐ scrap wood for temporary braces and stakes

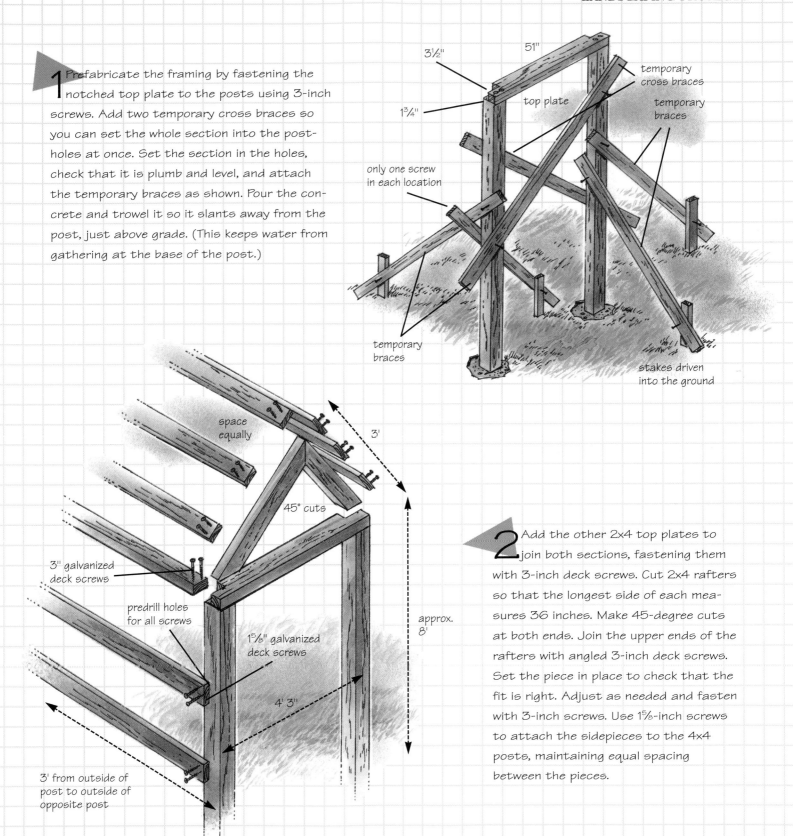

1 Prefabricate the framing by fastening the notched top plate to the posts using 3-inch screws. Add two temporary cross braces so you can set the whole section into the post-holes at once. Set the section in the holes, check that it is plumb and level, and attach the temporary braces as shown. Pour the concrete and trowel it so it slants away from the post, just above grade. (This keeps water from gathering at the base of the post.)

3½"

51"

1¾"

temporary cross braces

top plate

temporary braces

only one screw in each location

temporary braces

stakes driven into the ground

space equally

3'

45° cuts

3" galvanized deck screws

predrill holes for all screws

1⅝" galvanized deck screws

approx. 8'

4' 3"

3' from outside of post to outside of opposite post

2 Add the other 2x4 top plates to join both sections, fastening them with 3-inch deck screws. Cut 2x4 rafters so that the longest side of each measures 36 inches. Make 45-degree cuts at both ends. Join the upper ends of the rafters with angled 3-inch deck screws. Set the piece in place to check that the fit is right. Adjust as needed and fasten with 3-inch screws. Use 1⅝-inch screws to attach the sidepieces to the 4x4 posts, maintaining equal spacing between the pieces.

221

LATTICE ARBOR AND FENCE

GETTING READY

- Lay out your arbor and fence line using stakes and a mason's line.
- Select rot-resistant or pressure-treated lumber. If you plan to paint the structure, prime the lumber before assembly.
- Check to be sure the overall fence height of 7 feet complies with local codes.
- Prepare a flat surface on which to build the arbor framing and fence panels

MATERIALS LIST

Arbor	4' fence section
☐ (4) 4"x4"x10' posts	☐ (2) 4"x4"x10' posts
☐ (8) ¾"x¾"x14'	☐ 4x8' lattice panels
☐ (2) ¾"x¾"x16'	☐ (1) 2"x4"x8' fence rail
☐ (2) ¾"x¾"x10'	☐ (2) ¾"x¾"x10' stop
☐ (6) 2"x2"x14'	☐ ready-made finials
☐ (2) 2"x4"x14'	☐ 2x6x6" finial base
☐ (3) 1"x8"x12' seat backing	☐ 1½", 2½", 3" galvanized deck screws
☐ (2) 4x8' lattice panels	☐ gravel or concrete
☐ (1) 1"x4"x8' splice	
☐ (2) 1"x2"x12' seat framing	
☐ 1½", 2½", 3" galvanized deck screws	
☐ ready-made finials, screw shafts	

This elegant arbor and fence can add a new dimension to your yard. Ideal for dividing a garden area from the open spaces of your lawn, this project is functional, yet decorative. The arbor and fence look intricate, but the construction is made easier than it looks by the use of prefabricated wooden or PVC lattice.

1 Frame the arbor using 2x2s and 2x4s. Drill pilot holes before fastening the joints with 3-inch galvanized deck screws. Cut the lattice panels to size. Sandwich them between the ¾x¾-inch parting stop with 1½-inch galvanized deck screws.

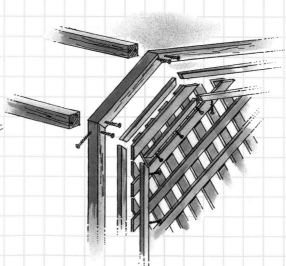

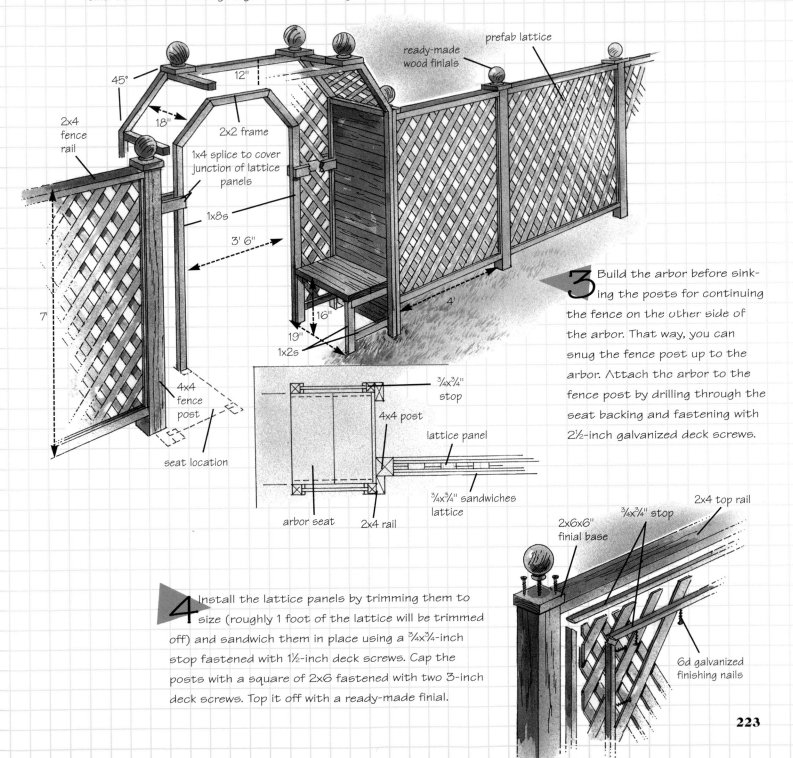

2 To build the fence sections, sink 4x4 posts below the frost line and anchor them in tamped gravel or poured concrete every 4 feet. Trim the posts to an even height, a maximum of 7 feet, to accept lattice panels trimmed and set vertically. Install 2x4 top and bottom rails using angle-driven 3-inch galvanized deck screws.

45°

12"

18"

ready-made wood finials

prefab lattice

2x4 fence rail

2x2 frame

1x4 splice to cover junction of lattice panels

1x8s

3' 6"

7'

4x4 fence post

seat location

16"

19"

1x2s

¾x¾" stop

4x4 post

lattice panel

¾x¾" sandwiches lattice

arbor seat

2x4 rail

3 Build the arbor before sinking the posts for continuing the fence on the other side of the arbor. That way, you can snug the fence post up to the arbor. Attach the arbor to the fence post by drilling through the seat backing and fastening with 2½-inch galvanized deck screws.

4 Install the lattice panels by trimming them to size (roughly 1 foot of the lattice will be trimmed off) and sandwich them in place using a ¾x¾-inch stop fastened with 1½-inch deck screws. Cap the posts with a square of 2x6 fastened with two 3-inch deck screws. Top it off with a ready-made finial.

2x6x6" finial base

¾x¾" stop

2x4 top rail

6d galvanized finishing nails

223

PICKET FENCE AND GATE

To increase privacy, buffer a prevailing wind, or simply add a homey touch, surround your yard with an ornamental and functional fence. This picket fence with its rounded gate will provide security for children and pets—and be a charming addition to your yard.

GETTING READY

- When planning your fence, keep in mind that many municipalities have special restrictions on fences more than 5 feet tall and maximums regarding picket spacing.
- Check for the location of underground utility lines.
- Consider renting a power auger to dig the postholes.
- Lay out the fence line, allowing 6 feet between posts. Place a stake where the center of each post will be.
- Choose cedar, redwood, or pressure-treated lumber.

MATERIALS LIST

- ☐ 4x4 posts
- ☐ 1¼" deck screws
- ☐ utility hinges and latch
- ☐ 1x4 pickets
- ☐ ¼"x3" lag bolts
- ☐ 1x8 for gate
- ☐ 2x4 rails
- ☐ post marker stakes
- ☐ ¼"x2" carriage bolts, washers, and nuts
- ☐ gravel or concrete

1 Dig postholes below the frost line. Set posts by first adding gravel to the hole, then plumbing and bracing the post in position. Pack gravel rather than soil around the post to inhibit rot, or set the posts in concrete.

2 Use a line level, or a 2x4 and a carpenter's level, to mark an even height for the posts.

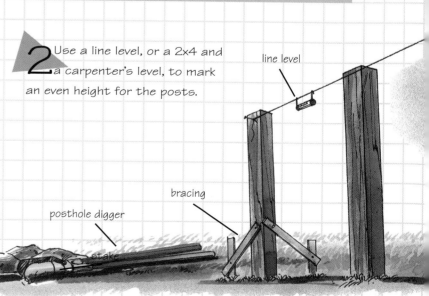

line level

posthole digger

bracing

stake

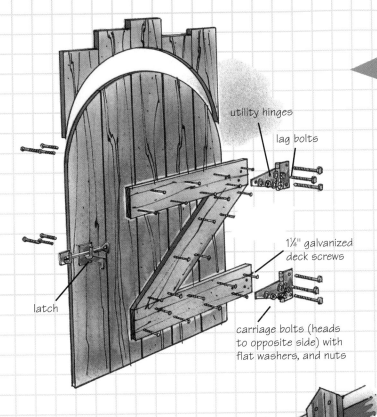

utility hinges

lag bolts

latch

1¼" galvanized
deck screws

carriage bolts (heads
to opposite side) with
flat washers, and nuts

spacer

3 Install the gate post to which the gate will be hinged (the hinge post). Build and attach the gate before setting the second post, the one against which the gate will close (the strike post). Build your gate by cutting 1x8s to approximate lengths, allowing for the the highest point of the gate. Lay the pieces on a sawhorse. Five 1x8s will yield a gate 36¼ inches wide. (Vary the width and height to suit your situation.) Attach the Z bracing, using 1¼-inch galvanized deck screws. Turn the gate over and mark the half-round top with a string and pencil. Cut the half-round with a jig saw. Attach the hinges with ¼x2-inch carriage bolts, flat washers, and nuts.

4 Galvanized deck screws are easier to install and more secure than nails. Caulk over the heads before painting.

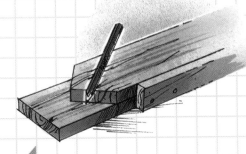

5 Make a template from a scrap of wood to mark the pointed tops of the 1x4 pickets before cutting with a jig saw.

6 Tack a 2x4 as a guide for setting pickets at the desired height. Use a spacer when attaching pickets. Typically, the spacer is the same width as the pickets but should be no more than 4 inches wide. Check for plumb every four or five pickets.

225

ARCHED GATEWAY

This handsome gateway is traditional in inspiration but has clean, elegant lines suitable for any contemporary setting. The ornamental detail of the posts is simpler than it looks—layers of dimensional lumber do the trick. However, the arch is a carpentry task best tackled by experienced do-it-yourselfers. Set the height and width of your gateway to suit your site, but be sure the gate opening is at least 3 feet wide and the posts are at least 5 feet high for adequate headroom under the arch.

GETTING READY

- Lay out the fence line and gate location with stakes and mason's line. Determine the gate dimensions and order materials accordingly. (The materials list assumes a gate 3 feet wide, with posts 5 feet high.)
- Cutting the mitered edges of the cornice trim is easier with a table saw, chop saw, or radial saw.
- Plan to build the picket gate first. It will be used as a guide for locating the gate posts.
- Complete the gateway before adding the picket fence. (For help on how to build the fence, see Picket Fence and Gate, page 224.)
- Check with your local building department for requirements regarding setback (the distance from public sidewalks, street curbs, and neighbors' lot lines), picket spacing, and fence height.
- Check for the location of underground utility lines before digging the postholes. Ask that stake markers be set.

MATERIALS LIST

- ☐ (2) 4"x4"x8' posts
- ☐ (1) 2"x4"x8' for furring out the posts
- ☐ (4) 1"x8"x10' for boxing the posts
- ☐ (1) 1"x12"x8' for boxing the post cornices
- ☐ (1) 1"x8"x10' cornice trim
- ☐ (2) 1"x4"x12' cornice trim
- ☐ (1) 1"x2"x12' cornice trim
- ☐ (1) 2"x8"x6' post cap
- ☐ (2) 2"x2"x8' post cap trim
- ☐ (1) 2"x8"x4' arch base
- ☐ (2) 1"x12"x12' for laminated arch
- ☐ (2) 1"x4"x14' for gate pickets (1½" spacing)
- ☐ (1) 1"x4"x12' for gate framing
- ☐ (1) 1"x2"x4' for gate stop
- ☐ 1 pound each, 6d, 10d galvanized casing nails
- ☐ 1 pound each, 1¼", 3½" galvanized deck screws
- ☐ 2 tubes each, construction adhesive, caulk
- ☐ hinges, latch for gate

1 On a piece of cardboard, mark a radius equal to the width of the gate opening. Cut the cardboard to make a template for setting the gate pickets. (Save the template for setting the height of fence pickets on each side of the posts.) Precut enough pickets for the gate and make a spacing gauge (see Picket Fence and Gate, page 224). Lay the pickets on two sawhorses and attach 1x4 bracing to the outermost pickets, making sure their tops are even. Set the other pickets in place so their tops just touch the arch template. Allow the bottom ends to run long. Double-check the squareness of the gate before adding the diagonal brace. When all the pickets are fastened, snap a chalk line and trim the pickets with a handsaw or circular saw.

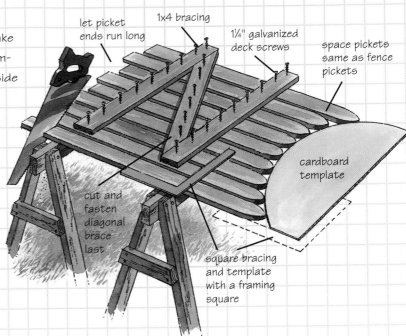

let picket ends run long

1x4 bracing

1¼" galvanized deck screws

space pickets same as fence pickets

cardboard template

cut and fasten diagonal brace last

square bracing and template with a framing square

note overlapping corners of 1x8 boxing

1x8 boxing slips over post and blocking

6d galvanized casing nails every 6"

2x4

space blocking at 3 to 4 points along post

4x4 post

2x4

3½" deck screws

2 Use the gate to position the posts, allowing for 2x4 blocking and 1x8 boxing, and ½ inch for swing clearance. Install the posts (see Lattice Arbor, page 222), setting the posts taller than needed. After the posts are in place, level across their tops and trim them 4½ inches lower than the final desired post height. Add 2x4 blocking to the posts about every 2 feet and where the fence rails or gate hinges will be attached. Use 1x8s to make the box, fastening the edges with progressively overlapping butt joints as shown at left. Trim the 1x8 box so that when slipped over the post, it will be 2 inches above the ground.

3 Slip the 1x8 box over the post. (Variances in humidity, warp of the boards, or finished dimensions may require you to back out screws and trim down the blocking.) Fasten the box to the 2x4 post blocking with 10d galvanized casing nails. Add 1x4 furring as shown, mitering the corners of the bottom trim pieces.

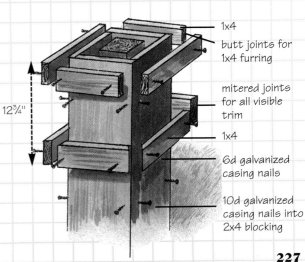

1x4

butt joints for 1x4 furring

mitered joints for all visible trim

1x4

6d galvanized casing nails

10d galvanized casing nails into 2x4 blocking

12¾"

227

ARCHED GATEWAY

4 Cut and fasten 1x12s to the 1x4s, positioning the 1x12s ¾ inch beneath the top of the post, leaving a ¾-inch reveal at the bottom of the cornice. Then add 1x8 flush with the top edge of the 1x12 and add 1x4 trim ½ inch below it, using 6d galvanized casing nails.

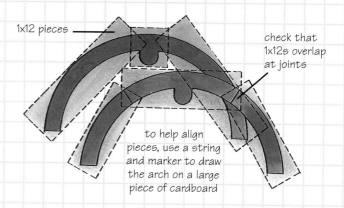

1x12 down ¾" from top of post

miter corners on all visible trim

1x8

1x4

1x12

½" gap

¾" above bottom edge of 1x12

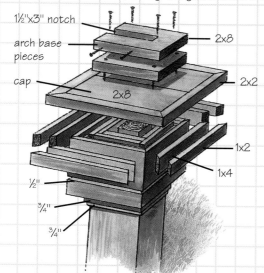

1½"x3" notch

arch base pieces

cap

2x8

2x8

2x2

2x2

1x2

1x4

½"

¾"

¾"

5 Add 1x4 and 1x2 trim to the cornice with 6d galvanized casing nails. Construct the cap by using construction adhesive to edge-join two 14½-inch pieces of 2x8. Trim the cap with 2x2 fastened with construction adhesive and 10d galvanized casing nails. Caulk the cap thoroughly. Cut two 10-inch pieces of 2x8 for each post, notching them with a jig saw to accept the base of the arch. Attach the cap with 3½-inch galvanized deck screws, drilling pilot holes to avoid splits. Attach the arch base pieces in the same way.

6 Measure the distance between the inside of both arch base pieces. Divide the distance in half to determine the inside arch radius. Lay out the sections of the arch (see Arched Arbor, page 216), making two sets of templates to cut the arch sections from 1x12s. For best results, trim the end of one section and place it over the untrimmed end of the next section before marking the joint.

1x12 pieces

check that 1x12s overlap at joints

to help align pieces, use a string and marker to draw the arch on a large piece of cardboard

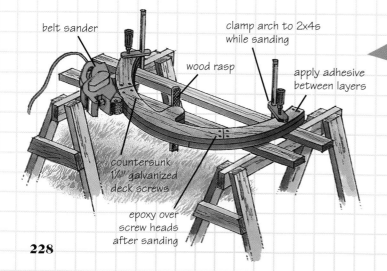

belt sander

clamp arch to 2x4s while sanding

wood rasp

apply adhesive between layers

countersunk 1¼" galvanized deck screws

epoxy over screw heads after sanding

7 Join the sections together to complete the arch, using construction adhesive and 1¼-inch galvanized deck screws. Predrill and countersink the screw holes. Use epoxy wood filler to fill any gaps and cover screw heads. With a belt sander and a wood rasp, smooth the edges of the arch. Position it on top of the posts in the notched base pieces. Anchor each end of the arch by drilling horizontal pilot holes through the notched bases and inserting four 3½-inch galvanized deck screws, two from each side. Hinge the gate to the posts (see Picket Fence and Gate, page 224) and fasten 1x2 stop with 1¼-inch screws.

GRILLWORK SCREEN

This grillwork screen can add interest to your home, increase privacy, and give climbing plants room to grow—all in one attractive structure. Built of 2x2s, 2x4s, 4x4s, and 1x6s, this project is simple and inexpensive to construct.

GETTING READY

- If next to the house, the height should approximately align with the top of a nearby window or door. Width can vary.
- Choose pressure-treated, cedar, or redwood lumber.

MATERIALS LIST

- ☐ (2) 1"x6"x12"
- ☐ (16) 2"x2"x8'
- ☐ (3) 4"x4"x14'
- ☐ (2) 2"x2"x10'
- ☐ (1) 4"x4"x8'
- ☐ (2) 2"x4"x8'
- ☐ 1 pound 3" galvanized deck screws
- ☐ 1 pound 2" galvanized deck screws
- ☐ gravel or concrete

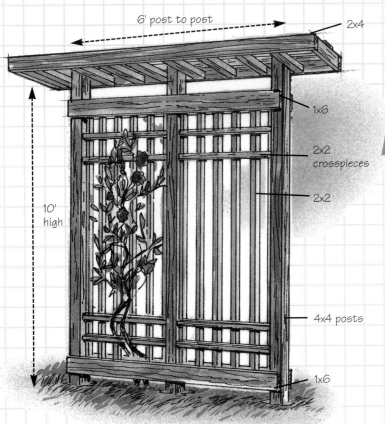

6' post to post

2x4

1x6

2x2 crosspieces

2x2

10' high

4x4 posts

1x6

1 Begin by digging all postholes below the frost line. Plumb and set the two outside posts in gravel or concrete. Level and fasten the upper and lower horizontal 1x6s, plumbing the posts as you go. When the 1x6s are in place, center the middle post and set in gravel or concrete.

2 Cut to size and fasten the vertical 2x2s of the grill to the upper and lower 1x6s, using 2-inch galvanized deck screws. Plan the spacing so that the holes of the grill are of a consistent size. Attach vertical 2x2s to the inner faces of the 4x4 posts. Cut and fasten the horizontal 2x2s. Cap off the grill with 1x6s at the top and bottom.

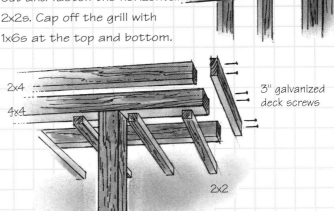

2" galvanized deck screws

1x6

2x2

2x4

4x4

3" galvanized deck screws

2x2

3 The top section is supported by a 4x4 attached to the posts with angled screws. The framework of 2x4s, to which the 2x2 crosspieces are fixed, is attached to it. Use 3-inch galvanized deck screws to fasten these pieces.

229

SCREENED SEATING AREA

If you've got an area of your garden that is too windy or too sunny, this project can transform it. The versatile unit provides a shady and sheltered place to sit, a good setting for potted plants that need partial shade, and a trellis for climbing vines. It also can screen for privacy or hide a utility area. Though fairly complex, this project is within the reach of a do-it-yourselfer with some carpentry experience.

MATERIALS LIST

- ☐ (4) 4"x4"x8' posts
- ☐ (2) 4"x4"x12' outside posts
- ☐ (12) 2"x4"x12' framing
- ☐ (3) 4x8' lattice panels
- ☐ (12) 2"x4"x12' lattice frame
- ☐ (5) 2"x6"x12' bench seat
- ☐ (3) 2"x6"x14' cap rails
- ☐ (17) 8"x12' lap siding
- ☐ (2) 1"x1"x8' trim
- ☐ (1) 1"x2"x6' trim
- ☐ 5 pounds 3" galvanized deck screws
- ☐ 2 pounds 1⅝" galvanized deck screws
- ☐ 1 pound 4d galvanized siding nails
- ☐ gravel and concrete

GETTING READY

- Use pressure-treated lumber for the framing and galvanized fasteners throughout. Consider cedar or redwood for finished surfaces.
- This unit can rest on the patio surface, but for greater permanence, set the outside 4x4s in concrete, just outside the edge of the patio.
- The number of sections can be extended to suit your site, but for strength and stability, limit each to 6 feet in length.
- Sketch a plan to suit your site. Keep in mind that the two side panels are at a 90-degree angle to each other.
- A power miter saw or radial saw is worth renting to make precise angle cuts.

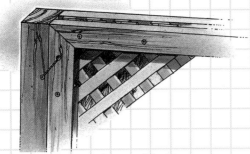

Use 3-inch deck screws in toenail fashion to attach the 2x4s to the posts. Use 3-inch deck screws to sandwich the lattice between the 2x4s.

1 Set the outside posts in concrete-filled postholes(see Arched Arbor, page 216). Then frame the back of the screen and install the 2x6 sills. Install the inside posts, letting them run wild. Cut all the posts to the same level height before you install the lattice frames. Next, install the seat framing. Fasten pieces of 1x2 and 1x1 trim where shown using 1⅝-inch galvanized deck screws. (Drill pilot holes for the screws to prevent splits.) You'll butt the siding to these pieces later.

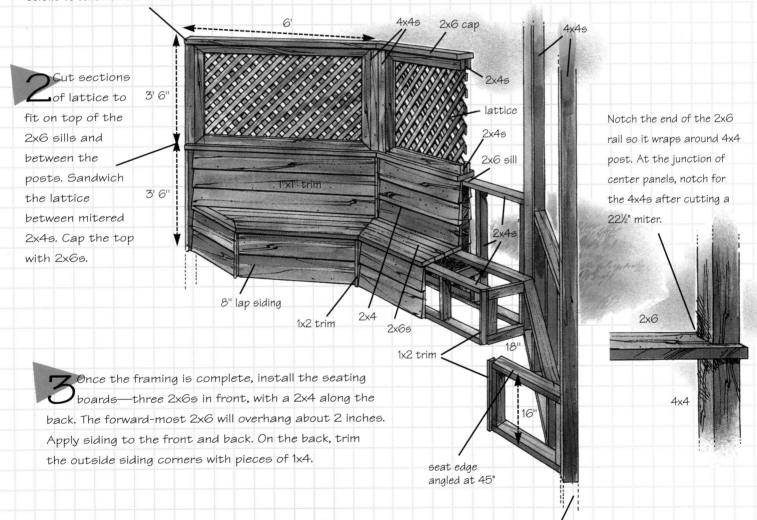

6'

4x4s   2x6 cap   4x4s

3' 6"

2x4s

lattice

2 Cut sections of lattice to fit on top of the 2x6 sills and between the posts. Sandwich the lattice between mitered 2x4s. Cap the top with 2x6s.

2x4s

2x6 sill

3' 6"

1"x1" trim

2x4s

8" lap siding

1x2 trim   2x4   2x6s

1x2 trim

18"

16"

3 Once the framing is complete, install the seating boards—three 2x6s in front, with a 2x4 along the back. The forward-most 2x6 will overhang about 2 inches. Apply siding to the front and back. On the back, trim the outside siding corners with pieces of 1x4.

seat edge angled at 45°

Notch the end of the 2x6 rail so it wraps around 4x4 post. At the junction of center panels, notch for the 4x4s after cutting a 22½° miter.

2x6

4x4

Attach all framing members with 3-inch deck screws. Drill pilot holes first, in toenail fashion.

2x6

4x4

When laying out the postholes, keep in mind that the two outer sections are at a right angle to each other.

231

MORTARED STONE WALL

A stone wall makes a statement that is at once both casual and stately. It has an aura of permanence, giving a timeless quality to even the newest landscaping. Stone is one of the most durable building materials. A simple stone wall does more than divide a garden or mark boundaries—it lends romance to a back yard.

GETTING READY

- Choose stones that blend well together in color and texture. You should get a good variety of sizes. You can use uncut rubble (pictured here), semidressed stone (roughly cut into rectangular shapes), or ashlar (stone that is carefully squared and trimmed).

- A mortar wall must be built on a firm foundation, or its joints will crack. Dig a trench about 6 inches wider than your wall. It must be deeper than the frost line, or at least 12 inches deep for a 3-foot-high wall. Tamp the gravel in the bottom of the trench, and pour at least 8 inches of concrete. Top off the concrete 2 inches below grade.

- Have the stone delivered as close to your building site as possible.

- Allow plenty of time for the project. Stone work is a matter of continual trial and error, testing to see which combination of stones works best.

MATERIALS LIST
- ☐ stone
- ☐ mortar
- ☐ concrete
- ☐ gravel

1 Build two batters of 1x4s to the dimensions shown, or varied slightly to suit your wall. For a wall 3 feet high, 18 inches is adequate. These templates can be leaned or propped at both ends of the wall. A string stretched between them acts as a guide for each course.

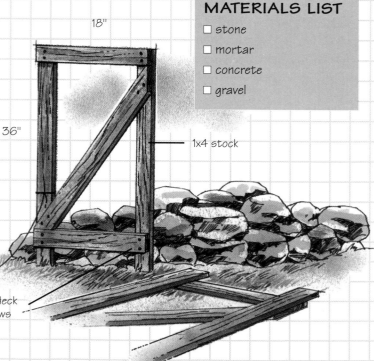

18"

36"

1x4 stock

1¼" deck screws

2 Set the first course in a 1-inch bed of mortar applied to the 8-inch concrete footing. Start with a tie stone, a stone that spans the width of the wall. Use larger stones for the faces, and fill in the middle with smaller stones and mortar.

tie stone

tie stone

wedges

tie stones

3 Dry-fit each successive course of stones, then make a mortar bed and carefully lay the stones. Place a tie stone every 4 feet or so, in alternating positions for each succeeding course. Use the batter board on the straight runs of the wall; freehand the curved corners. If a stone is squeezing mortar out of the joint, use wooden wedges to temporarily hold it up. Aim for fairly uniform joint spacing.

4 Rake the joints as you go, using a scrap of wood. Raking the mortar to a depth of 1 inch or even a bit more will add interest to the wall, producing pleasing variations of light and shadow.

5 Clean spilled or smeared mortar off the face of the stones as soon as possible, using a wet sponge. Immediately after raking, remove mortar crumbs with a whisk broom. After the mortar has dried, wash with plain or soapy water. Avoid using a wire brush or an acid solution, which can harm some types of stone.

233

TIMBER RETAINING WALL

On the face of it, this wall is a pleasing decorative feature that would be an asset to any yard. But underneath, it is a serious retaining wall that will stop an existing hill from sliding, or provide strong support for new landscaping. The hidden strength of the wall is supplied by deadmen, pieces that run perpendicular to the wall and extend into the hill behind the wall. These are attached to crossties, locking the wall into the slope.

GETTING STARTED

- In addition to the usual carpentry and digging tools, you will want a baby sledge for hammering the 12-inch spikes. (If you have trouble driving these without bending them, consider predrilling holes.)
- Consider renting a chain saw: Cutting 6x6s with a circular saw requires several passes. In addition, a chain saw will let you trim the timbers in place.
- If your slope is extremely irregular or large areas need cutting, consider hiring an earthmover.
- Be sure to install the drainage gravel and pipe as indicated, or water pressure (a massive amount can build up) will eventually cause the wall to buckle.
- Check your local codes before beginning. Some codes limit the height of amateur-built retaining walls.

MATERIALS LIST

- ☐ landscaping timbers or salvaged railroad ties
- ☐ 3" perforated plastic drainpipe
- ☐ gravel
- ☐ 12" spikes
- ☐ filter fabric or tar paper
- ☐ construction adhesive

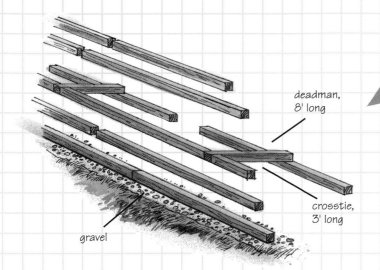

deadman, 8' long

crosstie, 3' long

gravel

1 Plan how your retaining wall will fit together, particularly the locations of the deadmen along the third course. Dig back any irregularities on the slope, allowing for at least 8 inches of backfill. Trench T-shaped cavities for the deadmen.

check for level after gravel is spread

2 Excavate a level trench that is 9 inches wide and an average of 6 inches deep. If necessary, dig behind the trench, so that there will be at least 8 inches for the drainpipe and gravel. Dig trenches for the deadmen. Spread 2 inches of gravel (more if you have soggy conditions) in the bottom of the trench.

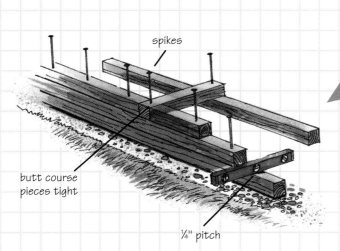

spikes

butt course pieces tight

¼" pitch

3 Lay the first course of timbers. These and all the other timbers should be level along their length, but should have a ¼-inch pitch to lean the wall into the hill. Apply construction adhesive between courses for added bonding and to keep water from seeping through them. Add the second course, attaching it with spikes every 3 to 4 feet. With the third course, install deadmen with crossties.

4 Install your remaining pieces, and provide drainage. Install the drainpipe (pitched ⅛ inch per foot) on the gravel bed. Backfill with gravel up to the top of the second course. Cover the gravel with filter fabric (or tar paper) and finish backfilling with soil.

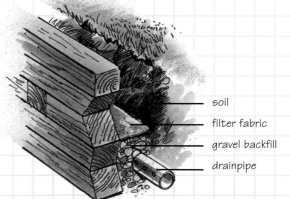

soil

filter fabric

gravel backfill

drainpipe

235

WRAPAROUND DECK

This wraparound deck, equipped with generous steps, is just the right size for intimate gatherings of family and friends. Because it is less than 19 inches above the ground, this deck needs no railing. (Check with your building department to confirm local code.) A windbreak trellis provides shade and privacy; the bench offers an inviting place for enjoying the outdoors. Each of these three elements is an individual unit that can be built separately or combined in ways to suit your own site.

GETTING READY

- Use pressure-treated lumber for the joists and posts, and cedar, redwood, or pressure-treated lumber for the decking and fascia boards.
- If your climate is prone to abrupt downpours, you may need a gravel-filled trench around the deck to collect runoff.
- In addition to basic carpentry tools, you should have a posthole digger, a shovel, and a container for mixing concrete.

MATERIALS LIST

- ☐ 4x4s for posts
- ☐ 2x8s for joists
- ☐ 2x6s for bottom-step joists
- ☐ 1x8 fascia board
- ☐ 1x6 fascia boards for bottom step
- ☐ 2x6s or ⁵⁄₄x6" decking material
- ☐ joist hangers
- ☐ angle brackets
- ☐ galvanized joist hanging nails or 1¼" galvanized deck screws

- ☐ 3" galvanized deck screws for header joists
- ☐ galvanized deck screws (2½" for ⁵⁄₄x6" decking, 3" for 2x6 decking) or 16d galvanized nails
- ☐ 1⅝" galvanized deck screws or 6d nails for fasciae
- ☐ redwood or cedar shims for the bottom step
- ☐ concrete and gravel for footings
- ☐ concrete tube forms for footings
- ☐ ⅜x5½" carriage bolts, nuts, and washers
- ☐ for a masonry house, ⅜"x4" lag screws with shields

1 Install the ledger board securely. For a frame house, screw into a joist, not just the siding. For a masonry house, install lag screws with shields every foot. Use batter boards and string lines to lay out your footings. Check for square using one or both of the following methods: (1) Mark a point on the ledger that is 3 feet from one end. Then use a piece of tape to mark the string line 4 feet from the ledger. When the distance between the two marks is exactly 5 feet, the line is perpendicular to the house. (2) Measure the diagonals of your entire layout. These measurements should be equal. Use a plumb line to mark footings every 6 feet. Dig and form up footings, and install posts (see Geometric Deck, page 242).

Allow for thickness of decking.

ledger

3'

5'

4'

Finished deck will be 2¼" longer on each end.

Use this post location as a reference point for positioning stair posts.

Plumb bob marks outside corner of post.

batter boards

237

WRAPAROUND DECK

2 Install the outside joists and header joist for the main deck, attaching the boards to 4x4 posts with carriage bolts. Check for level as you go. Cut the posts flush with the top of the joists (see Geometric Deck, page 242). Use the same method for the outside stairway joists. Mark for joists every 16 inches and install joist hangers.

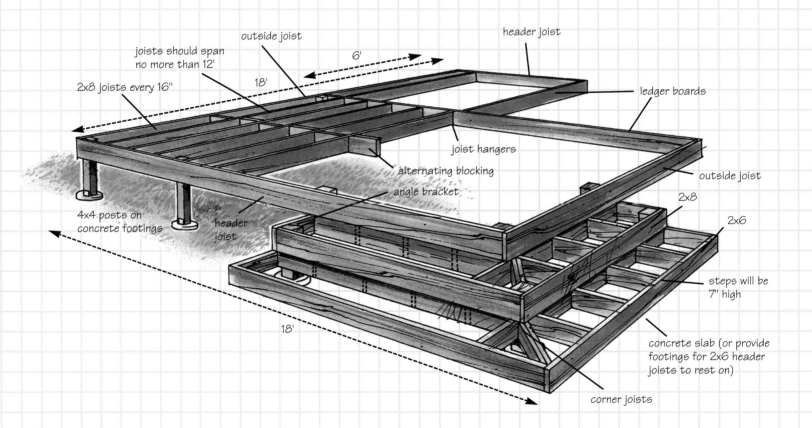

joists should span
no more than 12'

outside joist

header joist

6'

18'

2x8 joists every 16"

ledger boards

joist hangers

alternating blocking

outside joist

angle bracket

2x8

2x6

4x4 posts on
concrete footings

header
joist

steps will be
7" high

18'

concrete slab (or provide
footings for 2x6 header
joists to rest on)

corner joists

3 Site along each joist to see which way it crowns, or curves upward in the middle. Slip the joists into the joist hangers with the crowns up, and drive joist hanging nails or 1¼-inch screws in all the holes provided. In the middle of the joist run, install 2x8 blocking, using an alternating pattern to make nailing or screwing easier. On the stairs, install corner joists first, using 3-inch galvanized screws.

4 Wrap the outside joists and header joists with fascia board, using 1⅝-inch screws. Starting with the board closest to the house, install the decking. Measure equal distances from the house and strike a chalk line every four boards to keep the decking even. Some boards might be warped and will have to be forced into position. Use a pry bar to straighten them, being careful not to mar the top of the decking. Cut the first board (next to the house) exactly to length, but let the others run wild over the edge; you will trim them off later.

use 16d nails for spacers

predrill holes for screws near the edge

2x6 or ⅝x6" decking

fascia board

1⅝" galvanized deck screws

chalk line

5 To make the final cut, set the circular saw blade so it cuts through the decking plus ⅛ inch. Chalk a line and tack a guide board to make sure the cut is true. Don't force the cut; let the saw do the work.

239

WRAPAROUND DECK: BENCH

Narrow 2x2s rest on solid, square supports made of 4x4, making this bench an ornamental and inviting place to sit. It can be attached permanently to the deck or used as a piece of movable furniture.

MATERIALS LIST: BENCH
- ☐ (6) 2"x2"x12' for the seat
- ☐ (2) 4"x4"x10' for the supports
- ☐ (2) 1"x4"x10' cap
- ☐ 3 pounds 3" galvanized deck screws
- ☐ 1 pound 1⅝" galvanized deck screws
- ☐ (12) ¼"x6" lag bolts with washers

1 Cut pieces of 4x4 for the three supports. Countersink ⅞-inch bores ½ inch deep for the washer and head of the lag bolt. Drill pilot holes for the lag bolts. Place washers on the lag bolts and ratchet them tight.

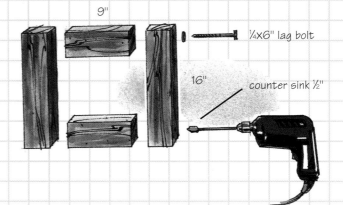

9"

¼x6" lag bolt

16"

counter sink ½"

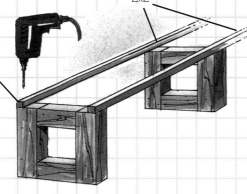

2x2

3" galvanized deck screws

2 Cut 2x2s to 6 feet in length. Attach the first and last pieces to the supports using 3-inch galvanized deck screws. Space the other 2x2s evenly, and attach. Align the ends flush with the edges of the supports. At the ends, predrill holes for the screws to avoid splitting the wood.

3 Wrap the bench with the 1x4 cap, using the 1⅝-inch screws. Corners can be butt joined or mitered. Fasten two 1⅝-inch screws at each post, and one every linear foot from end to end.

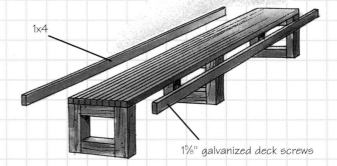

1x4

1⅝" galvanized deck screws

WRAPAROUND DECK: WINDBREAK

This attractive windbreak provides partial protection from prevailing weather, offers privacy from a neighbor's back yard, and can be a cool retreat ideal for dining. A baffle panel made of 1x4s forms the windbreak. Above it, a trellislike structure provides shade. This unit is primarily supported by the two rear posts, which require complete footings. The front posts rest on the decking.

MATERIALS LIST: WINDBREAK

- ☐ (2) 4"x4"x8' forward posts, (2) 4x4' rear posts: 8' plus the height of the deck above the ground, plus the posthole depth
- ☐ (7) 2"x4"x10' top pieces
- ☐ (2) 2"x4"x8' framing pieces for the windbreak
- ☐ (28) 1"x4"x5' slats for the windbreak
- ☐ (1) 2"x6"x8' support for the windbreak
- ☐ 2 pounds 3" galvanized deck screws
- ☐ 3 pounds 1⅝" galvanized deck screws
- ☐ concrete
- ☐ gravel

1 Begin by building the windbreak panel. Clamp the 2x4 frame pieces together. Mark the notches into which the 1x4 baffles will slide, using a scrap piece of 2x4 for the space between the slats and a scrap piece of 1x4 to mark the ¾-inch-wide cuts. Set your saw so it cuts ¾ inch deep. Make several passes with your saw for each notch. Clean out the notches with a chisel.

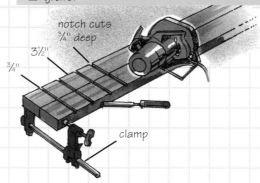

notch cuts ¾" deep

3½"

¾"

clamp

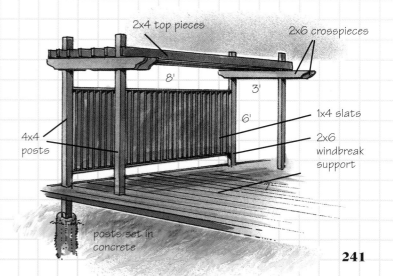

1⅝" screws

2 Cut the two notched 2x4 pieces to length so that the notches line up. Assemble the windbreak on a flat surface, fastening the 1x4s in place with 1⅝-inch screws. Drill pilot holes to keep the screws on course and to avoid splits.

3 Use the finished panel as a guide for setting the rear posts. Leave the posts long: They will be trimmed later. Install the 2x6 windbreak support and the baffle panel. Cut four 2x6 trellis crosspieces using the Square Arbor template shown on page 218. Attach these pieces to the forward (shorter) posts. Raise the posts in position, plumb them, and fasten the crosspieces to the rear posts. Attach the front posts to the deck with angle–driven screws. Trim the posts to height, and install the 2x4 top pieces.

2x4 top pieces

2x6 crosspieces

8'

3'

6'

1x4 slats

4x4 posts

2x6 windbreak support

posts set in concrete

GEOMETRIC DECK

A deck is a wonderful place to entertain or relax. Among the more popular do-it-yourself projects, a deck can be built by homeowners with a moderate amount of carpentry experience. This design accommodates minor variances in the footing locations and beam positioning so you can correct your work as you go. The angled deck section requires some additional work, but it is a popular and pleasing feature worth the extra trouble.

GETTING READY

- Use rot-resistant lumber throughout: pressure-treated lumber for the joists and posts, and redwood or cedar for the decking, rails, and fascia.
- Provide for drainage beneath the deck to avoid standing water or erosion.
- Check with your local building department about code requirements for footings, beams and joists, and railings. You will probably need a permit and have to undergo two inspections.
- In addition to basic carpentry tools, you will need a posthole digger, a wheelbarrow for mixing and transporting concrete, and a power miter saw or radial saw for making the angled cuts.

MATERIALS LIST

- ☐ (7) 4x4s for posts: size depends on height of deck
- ☐ (2) 10', (4) 12', (2) 14', (11) 16' 2x6s for joists and beams
- ☐ concrete and gravel for footings
- ☐ (7) tube forms for footings
- ☐ (7) post anchors
- ☐ 500 linear feet of 2x6 decking
- ☐ 40 linear feet of 1x6 fascia
- ☐ joist hangers: (14) regular hangers, (6) 45–degree hangers
- ☐ (4) angle brackets
- ☐ 20 pounds 3" galvanized decking screws
- ☐ 15 lag bolts and washers for ledger (with shields if you are attaching to masonry)
- ☐ 2 pounds 1¼" galvanized decking screws for joist hangers
- ☐ ⅜x8" carriage bolts, flat washers, and nuts

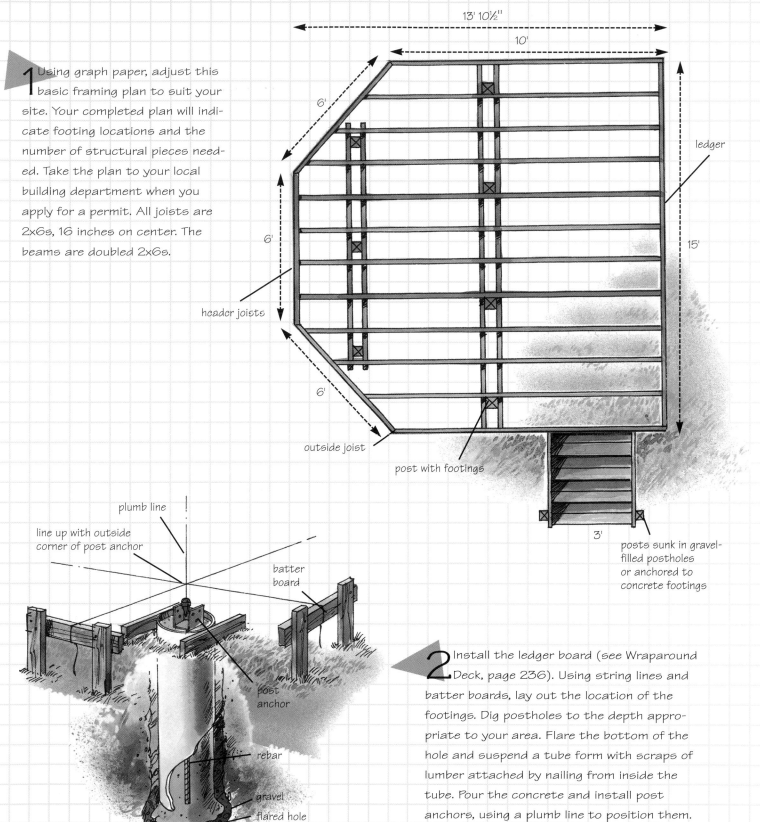

1 Using graph paper, adjust this basic framing plan to suit your site. Your completed plan will indicate footing locations and the number of structural pieces needed. Take the plan to your local building department when you apply for a permit. All joists are 2x6s, 16 inches on center. The beams are doubled 2x6s.

13' 10½"

10'

6'

6'

6'

ledger

15'

header joists

outside joist

post with footings

3'

posts sunk in gravel-filled postholes or anchored to concrete footings

plumb line

line up with outside corner of post anchor

batter board

post anchor

rebar

gravel

flared hole

2 Install the ledger board (see Wraparound Deck, page 236). Using string lines and batter boards, lay out the location of the footings. Dig postholes to the depth appropriate to your area. Flare the bottom of the hole and suspend a tube form with scraps of lumber attached by nailing from inside the tube. Pour the concrete and install post anchors, using a plumb line to position them.

243

GEOMETRIC DECK

3 Attach the 4x4 posts to the anchors and temporarily brace them, making sure they are plumb in both directions. Use a straight joist and a level to mark for the height of the posts. Rough-cut the 2x6s for the beam, leaving them a few inches longer than needed. Tack both beam members in place with 3-inch deck screws. Drill ⅜-inch holes for two carriage bolts. Fasten the bolts and trim the post with a handsaw. Build the second beam in the same way.

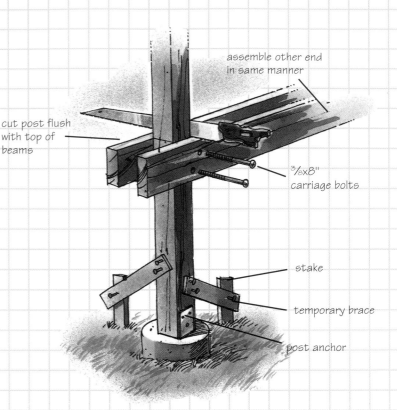

assemble other end in same manner

cut post flush with top of beams

⅜x8" carriage bolts

stake

temporary brace

post anchor

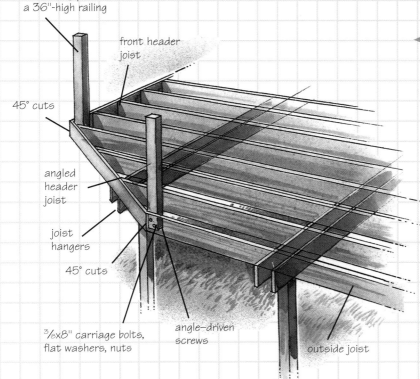

39" railing post for a 36"-high railing

front header joist

45° cuts

angled header joist

joist hangers

45° cuts

⅜x8" carriage bolts, flat washers, nuts

angle-driven screws

outside joist

4 Lay out the ledger for joists 16 inches on center and install joist hangers. Set the first outside joists in place and check them for square. Fasten them to the beam with angle-driven screws. Cut two 6-foot 2x6s for the angled header joists, trimming both ends at 45-degree angles. In addition, square-cut a 6-foot piece for the front header joist. Temporarily fasten the angled header joists to the outside joist and on the beam. Mark for interior joists. Use angled joist hangers for the joists that meet the angled header joists. When angled header joists are secure, fasten the front header joist in place. Cut railing posts and bolt them in position. When outside joists are in place, trim the beam ends flush with the joists. Install interior joists.

5 Apply the fascia to the header and side joists. Apply the decking with 3-inch galvanized deck screws, using a chalk line as a guide for keeping the heads lined up. Strike a chalk line for trimming the decking, locating the line even with the fascia. Trim it with a circular saw, the blade set slightly deeper than the thickness of the decking.

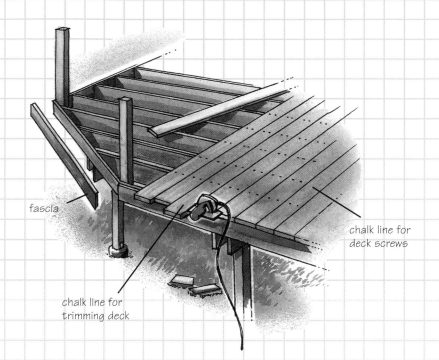

fascia

chalk line for deck screws

chalk line for trimming deck

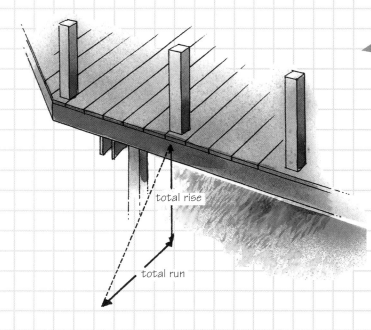

total rise

total run

6 To lay out your stairway, first measure the total rise—the vertical distance between the top of the deck surface and the ground where the stairs will end. Divide this number by 7 inches (which is an average vertical rise for a step) to arrive at the number of steps. Adjust the riser height until there is no remainder. That figure will be the rise for each step. For example, if the total rise is 30 inches, divide that by 7 to get 4, with a remainder of 2—so you will have 4 steps. To make things come out even, the risers should be 7½ inches (7½ times 4 equals 30). To figure the total run, multiply 11⅛ inches (the width of two 2x6s plus an ⅛-inch gap) by the number of steps.

245

GEOMETRIC DECK

7 Mark and cut the stringer. Use pieces of tape to mark the rise and run of the steps. Take into account the thickness of the treads—1½ inches. With 1¼-inch screws, attach tread cleats to support the bottom of each tread.

stringer

run

rise

cut off

cut off

8 Attach the stringers to the end joists with corner brackets. Now that the exact position of the stairs is established, set the stair rail posts in a posthole with gravel or anchored to a concrete footing. Level the stairs and attach the stringers to the posts with lag bolts. Add a suitable landing.

corner bracket

tread of two 2x6s, ⅛" apart

post set in posthole and gravel or concrete footing

MATERIALS LIST: STAIRWAY

- ☐ (2) 4"x4"x10' for stair posts
- ☐ 2x6s for treads: 6' for each step
- ☐ 2x12s for stringers: 2 pieces, length depends on rise and run of stairway
- ☐ tread cleats: 2 for each step
- ☐ 1 pound 1¼" galvanized decking screws
- ☐ (4) lag bolts
- ☐ gravel or concrete for footing

9 Plan on a railing of at least 36 inches in height. Cut two sets of upper and lower rails to sandwich the balusters. Cut balusters to size.

10 Using a 2x4 spacer and checking for plumb every fourth piece or so, install the balusters using 2½-inch screws.

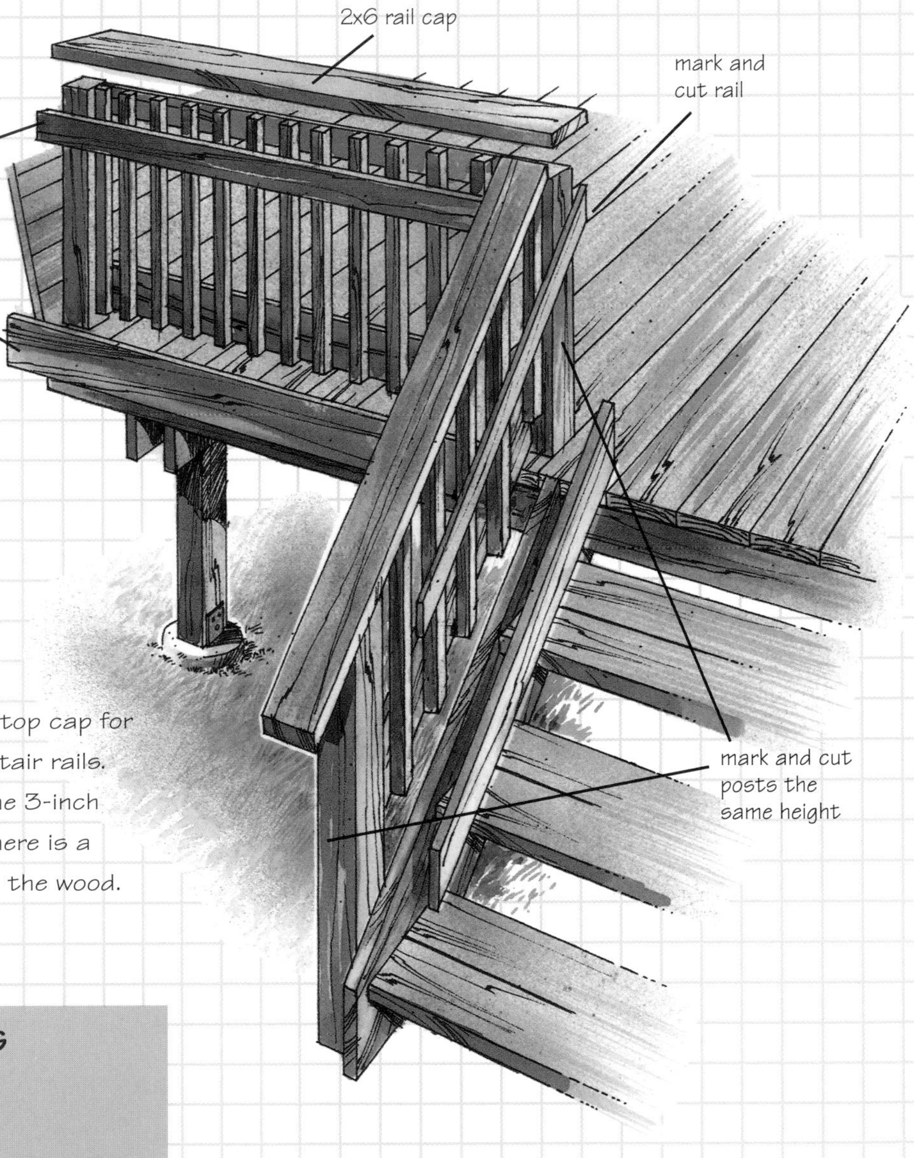

2x6 rail cap

mark and cut rail

1x4 top rails

1x6 bottom rails

11 For the trickier parts of the rail—especially where the stair rail meets the deck rail—hold boards in place and mark them.

mark and cut posts the same height

12 Install the top cap for deck and stair rails. Predrill holes for the 3-inch screws wherever there is a chance of splitting the wood.

MATERIALS LIST: RAILING

- ☐ (50) 2"x2"x12' for balusters, if spaced every 3½"
- ☐ (10) 1"x4"x12' for top rail
- ☐ (10) 1"x6"x12' for bottom rail
- ☐ (5) 2"x6"x12' for rail cap
- ☐ (24) ⅜x4½" lag screws with flat washers
- ☐ 5 pounds 2½" galvanized deck screws

CURVED BRICK PATIO

A rounded brick patio complements most any land-scaping scheme, adding a gracious old-world charm. Set in sand, this brick patio requires few tools and can be excavated by hand. The pattern shown requires almost no brick cutting. Setting the bricks requires only patience and a steady eye.

GETTING READY

- Lay out the patio area and excavate 7 inches below grade to allow for the sand base (3 inches deep) and the thickness of the bricks (4 inches).
- Plan to slope the patio away from the house, at an incline of 1 inch for every 4 feet (¼ inch per foot).
- In addition to carpentry tools for building the guide edge, you'll need a level, a baby sledge, and a brickset.

MATERIALS LIST

- ☐ 1 ton of sand for each 200 square feet of patio
- ☐ weed barrier: PVC sheeting or weed-block fabric
- ☐ 4-inch-wide ¼" hardboard strips for guide edging
- ☐ 2x2 stakes
- ☐ 2x4 guide boards
- ☐ 2x6 screed
- ☐ 1-inch deck screws
- ☐ builder's shims
- ☐ SW (severe weather) brick

1 Set the hardboard guide edging in place, leveling it as you go. Stakes seldom pound in exactly where you want them, so have builder's shims handy to help position the guide edging. Use 1-inch deck screws instead of nails to avoid misaligning the edging as you attach it to the stakes. Line the whole area with weed barrier. Install a 2x4 pivot base for the screed, staking the 2x4 at the desired height of the finished sand base. Notch one end of the screed to ride along the top edge of the hardboard guide edging as you smooth the sand. (Make the notch about 4 inches long to allow for variation in the form.) The depth of the notch should be equal to the thickness of the brick. Enlist an assistant to help you screed. Pivoting off the 2x4 base, screed the sand as smoothly as possible.

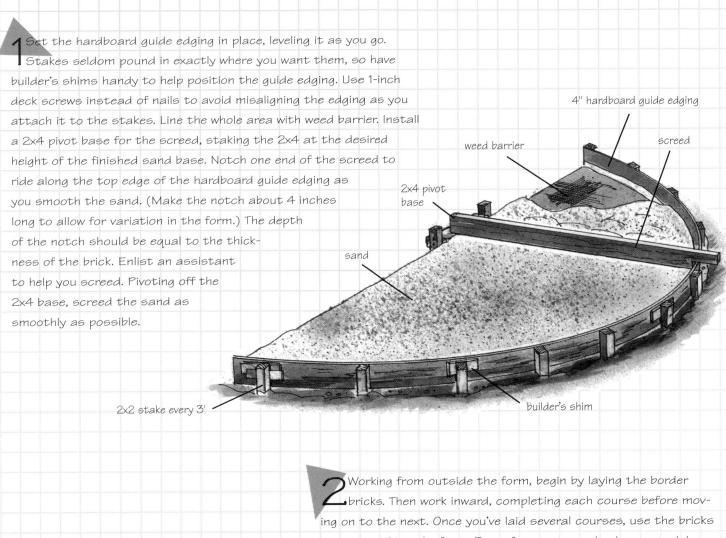

4" hardboard guide edging

weed barrier

screed

2x4 pivot base

sand

2x2 stake every 3'

builder's shim

2 Working from outside the form, begin by laying the border bricks. Then work inward, completing each course before moving on to the next. Once you've laid several courses, use the bricks as your working platform. Every few courses, check your work by scribing an arc with a string and stick compass attached to the pivot base. (For information on how to cut bricks, see Brick Raised Bed, page 274.) After the bricks are laid, brush sand into the cracks, moisten the patio gently, and brush in more sand where needed. Remove the form and fill in firmly with soil.

string and stick compass

TILE PATIO

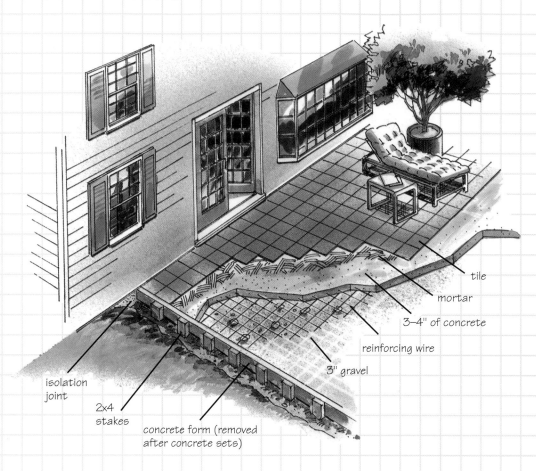

isolation joint

2x4 stakes

concrete form (removed after concrete sets)

3" gravel

reinforcing wire

3–4" of concrete

mortar

tile

Beautiful, long-lasting, and low-maintenance, tile makes an ideal surface for patios. A wide variety of colors, shapes, and textures is available to suit your taste and complement your yard. Tiles that are at least ¾ inch thick can be set in sand, in the same way as bricks (see Brick Path, page 206). However, all types of tile are more stable when applied to a concrete base. If you have an existing concrete slab that is smooth and properly sloped for drainage, you can skip the labor-intensive step of installing the concrete base. Otherwise, a permanent tile patio begins with pouring a concrete slab.

GETTING READY

- Determine the width, length, and depth of your patio slab. Give this information to your material supplier for estimating gravel and ready-mixed concrete.
- Schedule the concrete delivery carefully. If you have to pour a section at a time or if you have to wheelbarrow the concrete to the site, the driver will need to wait, and this will cost additional money.
- You'll need these special tools: wheelbarrow, hand tamper (or rent a power tamper), line level, concrete hoe, large hand float and/or bull float, tile cutter, notched tiling trowel, rubber mallet, and grout float.

MATERIALS LIST

- ☐ gravel: for a 3"-deep bed
- ☐ concrete: for a 4"-thick slab
- ☐ reinforcing wire mesh
- ☐ isolation joint material
- ☐ 2x4s and 2x8s to make stakes and build forms
- ☐ 3 pounds 3" drywall screws for forms
- ☐ tile (figure 15% waste allowance)
- ☐ mortar ("thin set" suits most tiles, but double-check with your tile supplier)
- ☐ grout

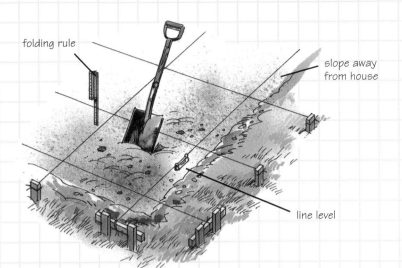

folding rule

slope away
from house

line level

1 Excavate the site to accommodate gravel, concrete, and tile.
In addition to batter-board lines
(see Geometric Deck page 242),
use a series of string lines to
gauge depth. Set the strings to
indicate the slope needed for
drainage—¼ inch per foot.

hand tamper

interior guide board,
spaced no more than 8'

pound stakes below
top of form every 1'

plywood ramp

2 Build a form of 2x8s, using 2x4 stakes.
If the patio is more than 8 feet wide,
install an interior guide board (called a stop
board). Spread 3 inches of gravel in the bottom of the bed. Cut reinforcing wire to fit,
then raise it above the gravel with stones. If
possible, have the concrete truck dump
directly into the form. If that is not possible,
construct a clear path with wide boards and
wheelbarrow the concrete in.

Remove interior guide
board once the first sec-
tion is filled, smoothed,
and has begun to set.

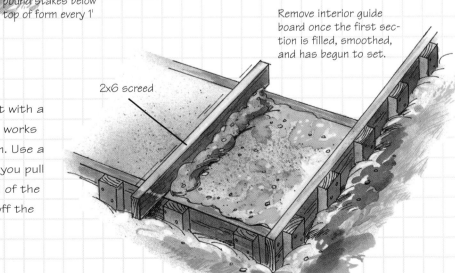

2x6 screed

3 Once a section is filled, level it with a
screed—a long, straight 2x6 works
well. This is a two-person operation. Use a
sawing, back-and-forth motion as you pull
the screed toward you. At the end of the
pull, the excess will slop over and off the
edge of the form.

TILE PATIO

4 Use a darby and/or a bull float to smooth the concrete. You do not have to achieve a completely smooth, finished surface, but the slab should be free of bumps and waves. Allow the concrete to set for five days before proceeding with the tiling.

darby

bull float

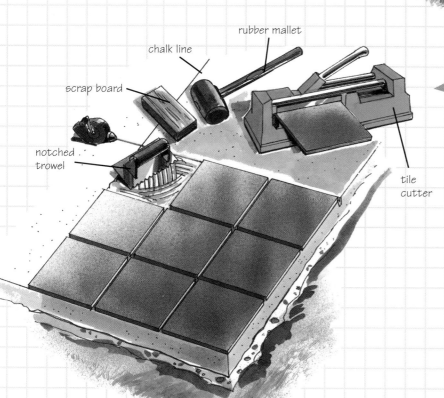

rubber mallet

chalk line

scrap board

notched trowel

tile cutter

5 Lay out two perfectly perpendicular lines to serve as starting points for your tiles. Mix the mortar according to directions and apply it with a notched trowel, taking care not to obliterate your lines. Set the tiles using spaces between the tiles to ensure the distance between tiles is consistant. Stand back and sight along the lines to check that they are evenly spaced. Gently tap tiles in place with a board and rubber mallet. Check that the tile surfaces are level with each other. Use a tile cutter for all straight cuts. Take the grout lines into account when measuring for the cuts.

6 Allow 24 hours for the mortar to set. Then apply the grout, using a circular motion with a grout float. Clean off excess immediately by dragging a heavy, damp towel across the surface. After the surface dries, clean the tile again using a large, damp sponge.

grout float

sponge

To build your own shady retreat, first choose a tree where you would like to sit—in a quiet, secluded area, maybe overlooking a favorite part of the yard. The tree should not be tilted too much and should not have many visible roots. The method of construction is to first build the bench in two sections, then to locate the postholes by holding the bench temporarily in place.

GETTING READY

- Purchase or rent a power miter box or radial saw—something that can make precise 30-degree cuts.
- Measure your tree's diameter 18 inches from the ground to determine the inside dimension of the bench.
- Use pressure-treated lumber for the posts and supports, and cedar, redwood, or pressure-treated lumber for the seat pieces.
- Draft at least one helper for the final assembly.

MATERIALS LIST

- ☐ 4x4 posts
- ☐ 2x4s for seats and supports
- ☐ 3" galvanized deck screws
- ☐ 5" hex bolts, nuts, and washers
- ☐ gravel

1 Put together six bench supports, using 2x4 pieces and screws. The faces of these will show, so make sure the ends of the three pieces are evenly cut and flush.

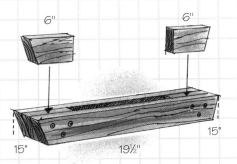

6" 6"

15° 15°

15° 19½"

TREE BENCH

2. Cut six pieces of 2x4 to be used as the seat pieces closest to the tree. The measurement of the longest side will equal the diameter of your tree. (If you have a fast-growing tree, make them 2 inches longer.) With two helpers, hold up all six pieces around the tree to make sure they are the right size.

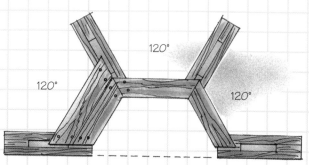

120°   120°   120°

align these pieces against
a basement or garage wall

length of this side equals
the diameter of your tree

30°   30°

3. On a large, flat surface, lay out the first bench section, using four seat supports and three of the bench pieces that you have just cut. Adjust them so that all angles are equal. Do not assemble yet.

4. Trim the rest of the boards, using the already-cut boards as guides. After positioning them tightly, install them with 3-inch galvanized deck screws.

at least 3" back
from edge

5. Build the second section. This will only have two bench supports, so screw pieces of 2x4 onto the bottom of each end for temporary support.

6 Set the two sections in place by resting them on chairs. When the whole assembly is positioned correctly, hang a plumb line from the center of each bench support, and dig up a bit of turf to mark each posthole. Shift the whole assembly to avoid large, exposed roots.

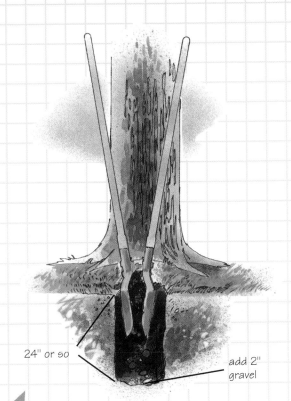

24" or so

add 2"
gravel

7 Dig your postholes. You will probably run into underground roots. Do not cut large roots, or you may kill the tree. As a general rule, any root less than 1 inch in diameter can be cut. Some postholes—no more than three—can be left shallow. Shorten the posts accordingly. Be sure the holes are wide enough.

8 Cut six 4x4 posts to the correct length—the depth of the hole plus 16 inches. Cut a tenon on one end so that the post will fit into the bench support. With your bench sections upside down, install each post, fastening it securely with a 5-inch hex bolt, a washer, and a nut.

tenon
1½"

3½"

9 Set the section with four bench supports in the postholes first. Then lower the other section into place. Make adjustments until the bench is level all around. Install the final screws, set the posts into the holes and tamp in place.

STONE TREE BORDER

This timeless-looking stone border adds an attractive feature and valuable planting area to your landscape. If you've ever wanted to build with stone, this is a doable project for beginners. It only requires patience in fitting the stones well and a strong back.

GETTING READY

- You can use almost any type of stone. Often, locally quarried stone is the most affordable.
- Plan on limiting the wall to no more than 2 feet high.
- Have the materials delivered as close to the site as possible.

MATERIALS

- ☐ ⅛" hardboard
- ☐ 1x4 stakes
- ☐ 1" deck screws
- ☐ gravel
- ☐ concrete
- ☐ stone
- ☐ mortar

1 Position a garden hose to mark your footing. Pour flour on the hose, and when you pick up the hose, you will have a clear line. Dig a 6-inch-deep footing 18 inches wide. Caution: Do not dig any deeper than 6 inches.

2 Add 3 inches of gravel and tamp smooth. Pour a 2-inch concrete footing over the gravel, keeping the top of the footing just below grade. Next, build a form out of strips of ⅛-inch hardboard. Cut the strips so they are a couple of inches lower than the final height of the wall. Pound in 1x4 stakes every foot or so. Fasten the joining ends of the hardboard with 1-inch screws and pieces of 1x4.

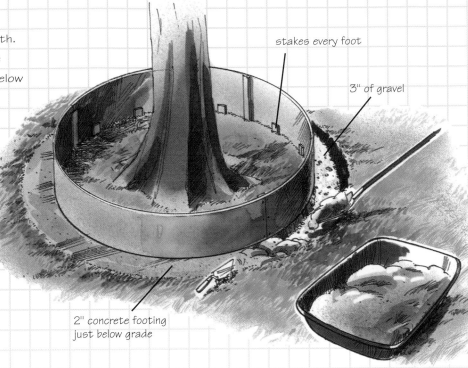

stakes every foot

3" of gravel

2" concrete footing just below grade

3 After you have determined where each stone will fit, wet the stone and, with mortar, butter the sides that will rest on the footing or touch stones that are already in place. Don't apply too much mortar at this point—after all the stones are set, you will fill in the spaces.

pointed trowel

mortar board

1" batter

tie stones every 4'

4 Your wall should be battered—its face should lean inward. For a 2-foot wall, maintain a 1-inch batter. When possible, use larger stones at the bottom and smaller ones near the top.

WINDOW BOX AND PLANTER

A dull entryway or empty patio springs to life with the addition of a flower-filled planter. Window boxes lend color and interest to lackluster windows. Such touches are easy to add to your home—ideal projects for budding carpenters. Here are a window box and a planter designed to hold potted plants for easy cultivation and maintenance.

GETTING READY

- Have on hand basic carpentry tools such as a circular saw with a combination blade, square, hammer, tape measure, drill and drill bits, block plane, and sandpaper.
- Measure your windows from the outside edges of the window molding to determine the length for the window box. Adapt the planter design to suit your space.
- Use redwood, cedar, or pressure-treated lumber.

MATERIALS LIST: WINDOW BOX

- ☐ 1x3 for top edging
- ☐ 1x2 for decorative border
- ☐ 1x8 for front, back, ends, and bottom
- ☐ 1x2 for backer strips
- ☐ 2x2 for brackets
- ☐ 6d galvanized box nails
- ☐ 3", 2" galvanized deck screws

1 Cut the 1x8 bottom and sides to a length equal to the width of your window, measuring from the outside edge of the trim on both sides of the window. Drill ½-inch weep holes every 6 inches, centered along the bottom piece.

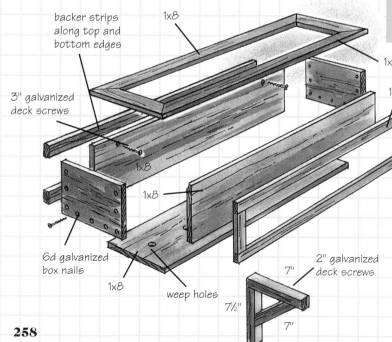

backer strips along top and bottom edges

1x8

1x3

1x2

3" galvanized deck screws

1x8

1x8

6d galvanized box nails

1x8

weep holes

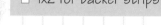

7"

2" galvanized deck screws

7½"

7"

2 Nail the sides to the bottom, drilling pilot holes and using 6d galvanized box nails. Nail the end pieces in place, again drilling pilot holes before nailing to avoid splits.

3 Cut and nail in place the front trim and top edging. Construct two brackets out of 2x2. Attach them to the house so the window box is just beneath the windowsill, using 3-inch galvanized deck screws (for wood siding) or masonry screws and anchors (for brick). Set the box on the brackets and attach it with 2-inch deck screws.

MATERIALS LIST: PLANTER BOX

- ☐ 1x8 for the sides
- ☐ 2x4 framing
- ☐ 2x2 framing
- ☐ 1x3 rim
- ☐ ½-inch exterior plywood for the bottom
- ☐ 6d galvanized box nails
- ☐ 3" galvanized deck screws

GETTING READY

- You can enlarge this design to suit your space, but add a 2x2 cross-brace at the bottom if you make it 3 or more feet wide. If you enlarge the box, try to do so by 7½-inch increments—the width of a 1x8. That will spare you having to rip the planks to size.
- Choose lumber that won't rot easily: cypress, redwood, cedar, or pressure-treated stock.

1 Construct the framing sections of 2x2s and 2x4s. Cut the bottom and drill two rows of ½-inch weep holes every 6 inches. Attach the bottom to the 2x2 frame with 6d galvanized nails.

2 Cut the sidepieces to length, trimming the leg pieces at a 45-degree angle so they have 1½-inch feet. Fasten the sidepieces to the frame sections, keeping the bottom of the planter 3 inches from the ground.

3 Miter the top edge pieces and nail them in place. Nail into the 2x4 framing and into the sidepieces, aiming the nails at a slight inward angle.

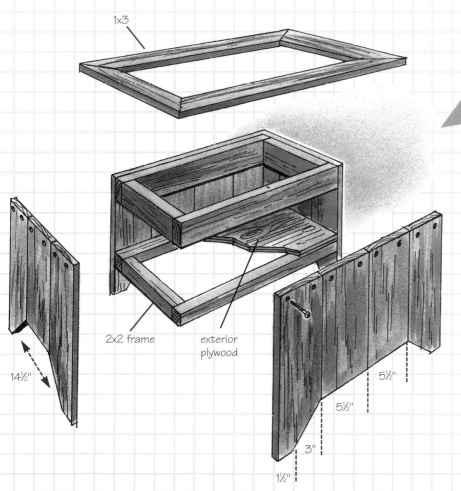

1x3

14½"

2x2 frame

exterior plywood

5½"

5½"

3"

1½"

LOW-VOLTAGE OUTDOOR LIGHTING

For a small investment of time and money, you can make your yard available for nighttime entertaining—and increase the security of your home. Low-voltage lighting systems are safe and economical. Because the cables carry so little voltage, many of the precautions required for normal electrical wiring are unnecessary, making installation quick and easy. You can choose to put the lights on a timer that will turn the lights on and off according to your specifications, or opt for a light sensor that will turn the lights on at dusk and off at dawn.

GETTING READY
• Low-voltage lighting kits are readily available at building centers and hardware stores. Equipped with transformers, these kits can be augmented with additional fixtures to suit the needs of most sites.

• If you do not have an exterior grounded outlet, hire an electrician to install a grounded exterior outlet equipped with a ground fault circuit interrupter (GFCI).
• A shovel and standard tools are all you'll need for most installations.

MATERIALS LIST
It is usually best to buy one of the many kits available. They will include most everything you need—a selection of light fixtures, cable, and a transformer. Some of the following types of lights will be in the kit; others can be purchased separately.

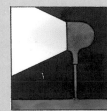

ENTRANCE
General illumination along walks and driveways

TIER
Along borders for a soft, decorative accent

FLOOD
Strong beam for backlighting or highlighting

GLOBE
General lighting without glare

MUSHROOM
Source of light is hidden for a soft, glowing effect

WELL
Upward beam for accenting trees, bushes, and buildings

1 Mount the transformer near a grounded exterior outlet. If you are installing a light sensor, mount it out of the range of street lights and porch lights—even the lights you are about to install. Locate it so it reads sunlight and darkness only.

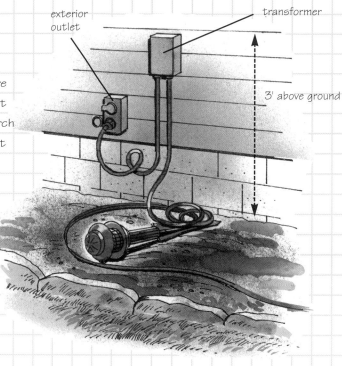

exterior outlet

transformer

3' above ground

2 Run the cable to the spot where you will install a light. Attach the fixture to the cable. (Some units, like the one shown, have clips that attach to the cable. With other units the cable comes already attached to the fixture.) Plug the system in and test it. (Cover the light sensor with tape to simulate nighttime.)

3 In flower beds, simply slip the cable under the soil or mulch. For places that will be walked on or mowed, dig a trench and bury the cable. To install each fixture, pierce a small hole 8 inches deep into the ground. Drive the stake into this hole, checking that the unit is plumb. Do not hit the light fixture with a hammer or exert undo force.

261

GARDEN POOL

GETTING READY

- Your pond should be sited on level ground, in an area that gets at least five hours of sunlight, accessible to a garden hose, and located where you can enjoy the view from your house, deck, or patio.
- Surprisingly, bigger is better for a backyard garden pool. Anything less than 2 feet deep and 8 feet in diameter collects heat and clogs with algae. In cold climates, dig an area at least 3 feet deep in which your creatures can live through the winter.
- Check before you dig. A quick call to your town's building department can help you locate water, gas, and electric utility lines.
- Lay out your pond by arranging a garden hose to mark the shape you want. Dust the hose with sand or flour to make a guideline for digging.

MATERIALS LIST

☐ PVC liner	☐ brick edging
☐ sand	☐ flagstone coping
☐ fine gravel	☐ round stones for pool bottom

For an appealing home for goldfish and aquatic plants, and an attractive feature of your yard, nothing beats a garden pond. It can be surprisingly easy to install and maintain if designed carefully. By excavating a hole, packing it with a layer of sand, and lining it with polyvinyl chloride (PVC) sheeting, you can create a pool of any shape you choose.

1 Dig the hole a minimum of 24 inches deep, sloping the sides slightly. Completely remove any large roots or sharp stones.

2 Use a level on top of a straight 2x4 to make sure that the pool rim is even. Pack the bottom and sides of the hole with 2 to 3 inches of moist sand. This helps smooth the sides and protect the liner from being punctured.

3 Position the PVC liner in the hole, leaving an extra 12 inches of liner all the way around the pond. Edge the pond with brick and trim the liner so the coping will hide it.

4 Create a base for the stone coping with a bed of gravel. Lay the coping in place so it extends 1 to 2 inches beyond the brick border. (See Flagstone Path, page 212, for how to cut stone.) Let the water stand for two days to disperse any treatment chemicals, then position pots of water plants, using stacked bricks to raise them to the proper height.

5 Set potted aquatic plants at the depth each requires. For example, water lilies should be set so the rim of the pot is 6 to 12 inches beneath the surface of the water. Gently set round stones on the bottom of the pond. When choosing aquatic creatures such as fish, snails, and tadpoles, check with your supplier about how many cubic feet of pond surface they need.

LANDSCAPING PROJECTS
PLAY CENTER

Be a star with your kids and make your backyard a place for safe fun by constructing this playground set. In a small space, this unit provides monkey bars, two swings, a rope climb, and a slide. The boxed-in areas on the ground can be filled with sand for safe landings. In the center of this play area, a 6x6-foot enclosed fort area makes a great place for safe fantasy play, as well as a fun spot for kids' lunches.

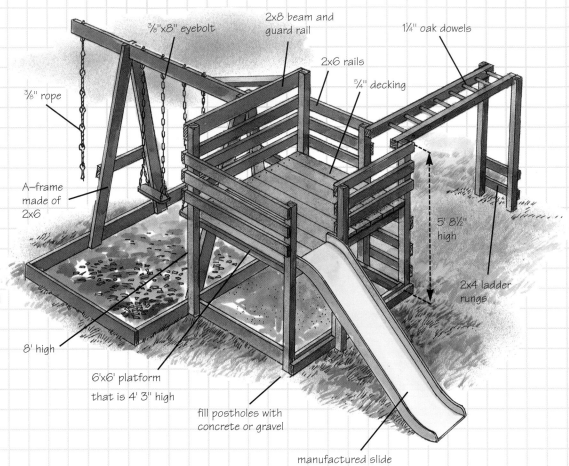

⅜"x8" eyebolt

2x8 beam and guard rail

1¼" oak dowels

2x6 rails

⅝" decking

⅜" rope

A–frame made of 2x6

5' 8½" high

2x4 ladder rungs

8' high

6'x6' platform that is 4' 3" high

fill postholes with concrete or gravel

manufactured slide

GETTING READY

• Choose redwood or pressure-treated lumber for this project. (Cedar is too weak.) If you are using pressure-treated lumber, check with your supplier to make sure it is dry and safe for kids. Pick each piece of lumber yourself, checking for cracks and splinters. Keep in mind that you will have to sand until each piece has round, safe edges.

• There are kits available that include swings, slide, climbing rope, and special hardware.

• Excavate the site and install a weed barrier to keep vegetation from growing. If rainwater tends to puddle on the site, provide gravel beds for posts and the ground-level enclosures.

• You will need basic carpentry tools, including a 1¼-inch spade bit and a long ⅜-inch bit to drill through the 7½-inch width of a 2x8. A power miter saw will make it easy to cut clean, straight edges. A belt sander will help sand the lumber smooth.

• Sand the edges of all pieces before you assemble them. It will be more difficult to do so after the unit is assembled.

MATERIALS LIST

- ☐ (6) 4"x4"x10' for posts
- ☐ (4) 4"x4"x8' for monkey-bar members
- ☐ (10) 2"x6"x12', (2) 2"x6"x10' for rails, ground-level enclosures, platform joists, and A-frame support
- ☐ ⁵⁄₄" decking or 2x6 to cover 40 square feet
- ☐ (2) 2"x4"x8' for climbing rungs, bracing
- ☐ (1) 2"x8"x16' for the swings' beam and crosspiece
- ☐ (8) 1¼"x24" oak dowels for monkey bars
- ☐ 3" galvanized deck screws
- ☐ concrete and gravel for 2 postholes

- ☐ (5) ⅜x8" eyebolts with washers and nuts
- ☐ (4) ⅜x6" carriage bolts, flat washers, and nuts
- ☐ plastic slide (a 10-foot slide will be safer and slower than an 8 footer)
- ☐ 2 swings with chains
- ☐ ¾x10' sisal rope
- ☐ 1 ton of sand for each 200 square feet of play area
- ☐ weed barrier: PVC sheeting or weed-block fabric

1 After cutting the pieces and sanding their edges, construct two platform support units of 4x4s and 2x6s. Fasten them with 3-inch galvanized deck screws. Cut four pieces of 2x6 as shown and assemble the support frame. If the ground is uneven, you will have to dig under the frame and posts until the rails are level and the posts are plumb.

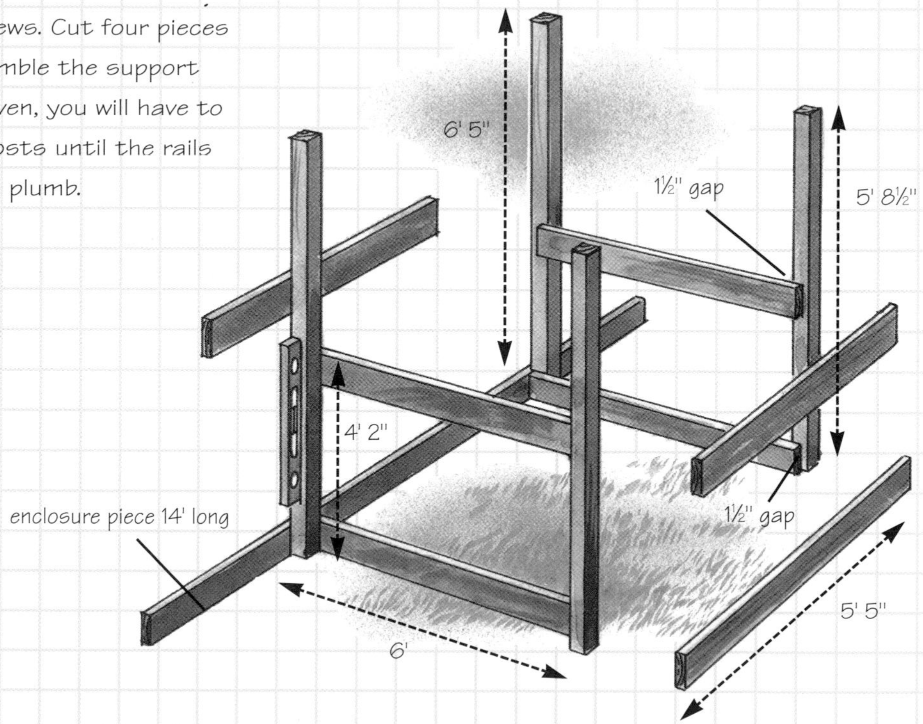

6' 5"

1½" gap

5' 8½"

4' 2"

enclosure piece 14' long

1½" gap

6'

5' 5"

PLAY CENTER

2 Install three 2x6 interior joists, 18 inches on center. Fasten the decking, leaving a ¼-inch gap between the boards. The structure will be wobbly at first but will firm up as you build. Add two posts, making sure you allow a 23-inch opening for the monkey bars and an appropriate opening for the slide you have purchased. Cut and install 2x6 railings, spacing them evenly and checking for level.

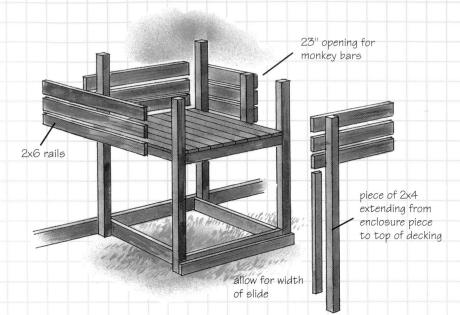

23" opening for monkey bars

2x6 rails

piece of 2x4 extending from enclosure piece to top of decking

allow for width of slide

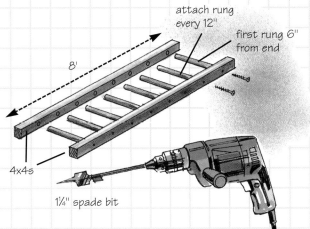

attach rung every 12"

first rung 6" from end

8'

4x4s

1¼" spade bit

3 Use a piece of tape to mark a 1¼-inch drill bit as a depth gauge for boring holes 1½ inches deep. Drill evenly spaced holes in both pieces of 4x4 as shown. Cut two dowels 19 inches long, fit them in place, and check to see that the finished unit will fit snugly between the posts on the platform. Cut the rest of the dowels and predrill all screw holes to avoid splitting the dowels.

4 Use countersunk carriage bolts to attach the monkey bars to the structure and to two posts set in postholes. Level the monkey bars before finally plumbing and setting the 4x4 uprights in concrete. Attach 2x4 ladder rungs with 3-inch galvanized deck screws, spacing them 12 inches from the top of one rung to the top of the next.

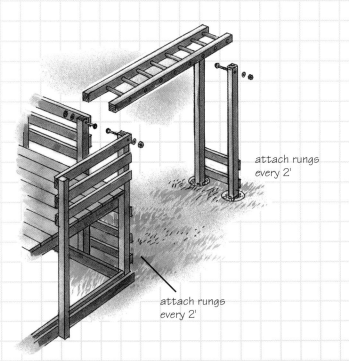

attach rungs every 2'

attach rungs every 2'

5 Cut a 2x8 to a length of 9 feet 7 inches (115 inches). With a long drill bit, drill down through a 2x8 and install eyebolts. (The measurements shown may change according to the swings you purchase.) Attach the 2x8 crosspiece with screws. Construct an A-frame support of 2x6. The beam should fit snugly into the top. Make the A-frame support a bit long so you can trim the feet until the beam is level. Screw the beam into the crosspiece, then add a 2x4 angle support. Complete construction of the 2x6 play area border. Either purchase a climbing rope with knots in it, or knot the rope yourself.

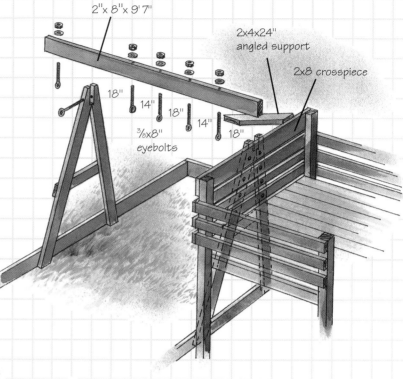

2"x 8"x 9' 7"

2x4x24"
angled support

2x8 crosspiece

18"

14"

18"

14"

18"

³⁄₈x8"
eyebolts

6 Attach the swings and slide according to the manufacturer's directions. Fill the two enclosed ground-level areas with sand. Check carefully for rough surfaces and splintering wood before allowing children to play on the structure.

GARDENING SHED

Tired of dragging gardening tools out of the garage each time you garden? This handy shed provides sheltered storage and working space close to where you garden. With every tool in its place, you'll find gardening more fun and less hassle.

GETTING READY

- The dimensions of this shed can be adapted to suit your site. Minimum floor area should be 20 square feet.
- Place the concrete-block footings in concrete and allow the concrete to set at least 24 hours.

MATERIALS LIST

- ☐ (3) 2"x4"x10', (1) 2"x4"x12' floor framing (pressure-treated)
- ☐ (8) 2"x4"x10', (16) 2"x4"x8' wall, roof framing
- ☐ 3 pounds each, 16d, 8d cement-coated common nails
- ☐ (2) 4'x8'x½" CDX plywood
- ☐ (5) 4'x8'x⅝" T-111 plywood siding
- ☐ (7) 1"x4"x8', (2) 1"x4"x10' corner trim
- ☐ (3) 1"x6"x8' for jamb and fascia
- ☐ premixed concrete
- ☐ concrete blocks
- ☐ flashing, felt, shingles, roofing nails
- ☐ 1 pound 3" deck screws

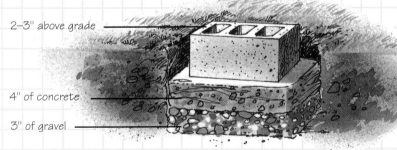

2–3" above grade

4" of concrete

3" of gravel

1 For each footing, dig a hole slightly larger than the concrete block and about 12 inches deep. Put in gravel, then concrete, and set the block in it. Check that the blocks are level with each other by using a 2x4 on edge and a carpenter's level to span across two blocks.

2 For ease of construction, fabricate the floor and wall frames on the driveway. Attach the floor frame by using 3-inch deck screws to fasten it to short 2x4s pushed into the holes of the concrete block. Attach the plywood floor. Then position the wall frames, check for plumb, and attach the side walls to the house with 3-inch deck screws if you have a frame house, or lag screws (not masonry nails) and shields for a masonry house.

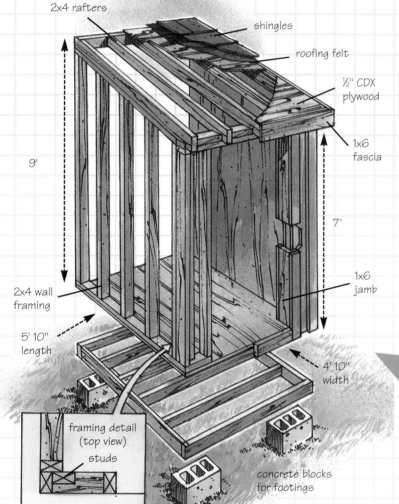

2x4 rafters

shingles

roofing felt

½" CDX plywood

1x6 fascia

9'

7'

2x4 wall framing

5' 10" length

1x6 jamb

framing detail (top view) studs

4' 10" width

concrete blocks for footings

3 Attach the single top plate to the wall of the house. Cut the first rafter so it fits snugly around the doubled top plate of the shed wall. Trim its tail end plumb. Then use it as a template for the other four rafters. Toenail the rafters in place.

4 If you don't want the exterior of your house to show inside the shed, cover it with a sheet of T-111 siding. If you wish to have interior walls, construction-grade CDX plywood is an inexpensive option.

5 Cover the exterior of the shed with T–111 plywood siding, or another type of siding that harmonizes with the siding on your house. Make sure it's snug against the house and no closer than 2 inches to the ground. Caulk between the plywood and the house.

6 Trim the corners with 1x4s. Use 1x6s to make an entry jamb. The door can be made using the same technique and hardware as the gate shown in Picket Fence and Gate, page 224. Cover the roof with plywood and add 1x6 as fascia. Apply felt, flashing (seal it to the roof with roofing cement), and shingles, allowing them to overhang the roof ½ inch.

MODULAR RAISED BEDS

Raised beds are an attractive and practical solution for small yards. They tame a rampant vegetable garden by creating neat compartments that are easy to weed, water, and mulch. And, as you add compost, peat moss, and other humus-building matter, the wooden sides keep the soil from avalanching away. Access paths between the beds allow for easy weeding and harvesting, and keep heavy footfalls from compacting deep-tilled soil.

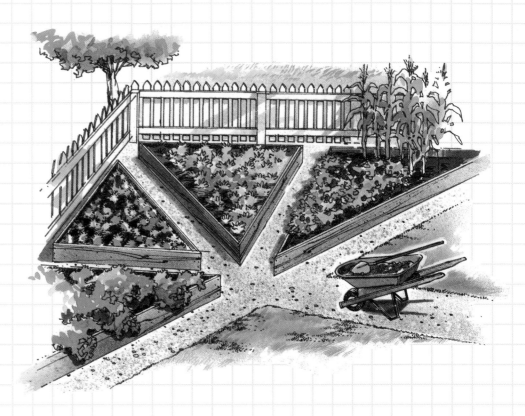

GETTING READY
- Choose pressure-treated, cedar, or redwood 2x10s. (If you choose pressure-treated lumber, be sure to wear a dust mask and eye protection while sawing.)
- Roughly grade the area for the garden so it is level. Use stakes and string to lay out each raised bed, making sure that the strings are 12 inches above the ground.
- Comfortable paths are at least 24 inches wide. (If you plan to have grass paths, set beds to make a path at least 3 inches wider than your lawn mower.)
- In addition to basic carpentry tools, you'll need a baby sledge, a rachet and sockets, and large C-clamps.

MATERIALS LIST
- ☐ construction-grade 2x10s
- ☐ 3x24" PVC pipe sections
- ☐ 3" galvanized deck screws
- ☐ ¼x5½" carriage bolts
- ☐ ¼" nuts, washers

1 Using the layout strings as a guide, cut the 2x10s roughly to length. With 3-inch deck screws, fasten the two pieces that form a 90-degree angle. Set the piece that forms the hypotenuse on top of the pieces and mark it for the angled cut.

fasten right-angle corner with 3" deck screws

mark for angled cut

2 Set your circular saw blade so it matches the angled mark on the hypotenuse piece. Mark a perpendicular cutting line and cut the piece to size. Drill pilot holes and fasten the piece in place using 3-inch galvanized deck screws.

PVC pipe 1½" beneath top edge of 2x10

trim excess 2x10 flush with outside edge

3 Set the enclosure on scraps of 2x4 and trim the excess 2x10 with a coarse-cut handsaw. Position the unit on the ground and pound 2-foot sections of 3-inch PVC pipe into each corner. If you are working with a large garden, install a pipe every 6 feet to keep the enclosure from bowing.

3" PVC pipe

⁵⁄₁₆" hole

¼x5½" carriage bolt, nut, and washer

4 Level the 2x10 frame, laying scraps of lumber and builder's shim to bring it to the desired height. Holding the frame to the pipe with a C-clamp, drill two ⁵⁄₁₆-inch holes through the 2x10 and PVC pipe. Insert two ¼x5½-inch carriage bolts at each stake, add a washer and nut, and tighten in place. Fill the pipes with gravel and top them off with mortar mix.

271

LANDSCAPING PROJECTS
BRICK RAISED BED

Building with brick can be pleasant work, but it takes some practice before you become proficient. This handsome wall will be strong enough for a planting bed up to 2 feet high. Anything higher requires a double brick wall. It will take a couple of weekends to become competent at bricklaying, but the results will be well worth the effort. The completed project will be a permanent landscaping feature you can be proud of.

GETTING READY

• Choose bricks that will survive well in continually wet conditions. Common brick may not be strong enough. Be prepared to give your material supplier the length and height of the wall you plan to build. If the bricks have holes in them, purchase special cap bricks for the top course.

• Arrange to have the bricks resting on a strong pallet near the job site.

• Consult your building supplier for the right mixture of cement, lime, and sand, or buy mortar mix.

• You will need a mortar board (a 3-foot-square piece of plywood nailed to two 2x4s works fine), a wheelbarrow or large container for mixing mortar, a mortar hoe, a brickset chisel, a mason's line with line blocks, a pointing trowel, a joint raking tool, and a joint pointer (either convex or V-shaped).

• Make a story pole—a length of 1x2 with evenly spaced lines marking the height of each course of bricks.

• Install a level concrete footing, combining a 12-inch-deep, reinforced, and concrete-filled trench twice as wide as the brick wall will be with concrete footings every 4 feet that extend beneath the frost line (see Geometric Deck, page 242).

1 Chalk a guideline to position the bricks on the center of the footing. Make a dry run: Lay out the bricks without mortar, spacing them evenly. This will tell you if you need to insert a short brick near the end of the run. If necessary, increase the spaces to avoid putting in a very small piece of brick. Mark the locations of the first and last brick.

⅜" gap (about the thickness of your little finger)

chalk line

2 Mix a small batch of mortar. Set the first two bricks, one at each end, laying down a 1-inch-thick bed for each. Check for level in both directions, tapping gently with the handle of your trowel to make adjustments. String a mason's line to mark the level of the first course of bricks. Hold the line in place with bricks.

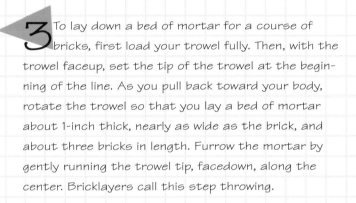

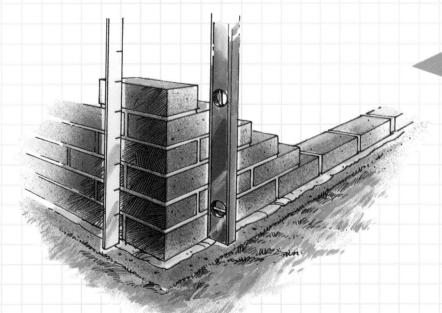

3 To lay down a bed of mortar for a course of bricks, first load your trowel fully. Then, with the trowel faceup, set the tip of the trowel at the beginning of the line. As you pull back toward your body, rotate the trowel so that you lay a bed of mortar about 1-inch thick, nearly as wide as the brick, and about three bricks in length. Furrow the mortar by gently running the trowel tip, facedown, along the center. Bricklayers call this step throwing.

4 Build the lead—the beginning point for your courses. This is six courses high, with each course half of a brick shorter than the one below it. (Remember that a brick is half as wide as it is long.) Level and plumb each course, and use a story pole to check for height. Lay down mortar and add the first course. Butter the end of each brick where it abuts another. Add the mortar by making a swiping motion along all four edges of each face.

BRICK RAISED BED

5 Duplicate the lead on the other end of the wall. String a mason's line as a course guide, using line blocks to hold the line flush with the face of the bricks. Using the line as a guide, fill in each course, remembering to throw, furrow, and butter. Cut bricks by first scoring a line around the brick. Then crack the brick using a mallet and a brickset.

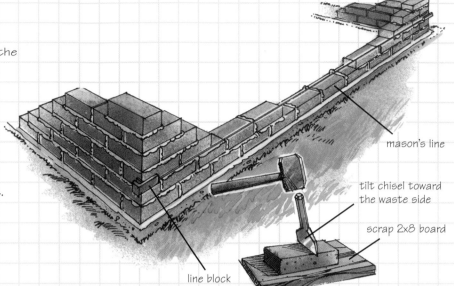

mason's line

tilt chisel toward
the waste side

scrap 2x8 board

line block

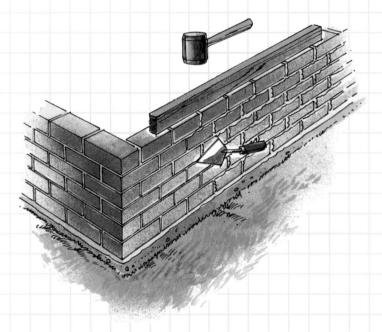

6 Continually adjust for level and straight courses, tapping gently with a mallet and 2x4. As you proceed, scrape off excess mortar with your trowel, taking care not to smear the bricks. Every so often, press the mortar with your thumb. If it feels firm and your thumb impression does not change shape, the joints can be finished.

7 Using a pointing tool, first smooth out the vertical joints, then the horizontals. Gently brush away excess as you work. Wash any smeared spots carefully with a damp rag—once the mortar has set, it will be difficult to remove.

LANDSCAPING TIMBER BED

Here's a quick way to give your backyard a lift, adding variety and interest while making future gardening tasks easier on your back. No fine carpentry is required to make the classy-looking bed—just a little heavy lifting and a couple of Saturdays.

GETTING READY

- Choose timbers that will last well in your climate. Pressure-treated landscaping timbers are commonly available in 8-foot 5x6s, 6x6s, and 6x8s.
- You will need a high-quality, ⅜-inch extension bit for boring through the timbers. A chain saw will make cutting the timbers easier, but be sure to take all safety precautions. Wear gloves and eye protection when cutting pressure-treated lumber.

1 Where the wood will rest on the ground, dig a level trench 2 inches wider than your timbers and about 3 inches deep.

2 Pour and level a base of gravel, making it nearly as high as the surrounding grade.

3 Lay the first course of timbers on the gravel. Bore ⅜-inch holes down through the timbers every 3 feet. Set precut 2-foot pieces of ⅜-inch reinforcing bar in each of the holes and pound them flush with the surface of the timber.

4 Attach the final two courses with 12-inch spikes, predrilling 3 inches into the timbers with a ¼-inch bit.

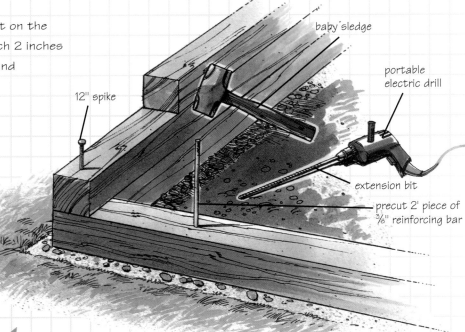

baby sledge

portable electric drill

12" spike

extension bit

precut 2' piece of ⅜" reinforcing bar

COMPOST CENTER

A simple wire compost bin can be built by wiring sections of fencing material to corner posts (pound 1-inch galvanized pipe into the ground to create the posts). With such a unit, lawn waste, vegetable scraps from the kitchen, and leaves can be returned to your soil rather than overloading the local landfill. Frequent turning, maintaining moisture about equal to that of a damp sponge, and adding occasional layers of soil will aid quick conversion.

Recycle kitchen and yard waste with a soil-building compost center. Whether you choose to put up a simple wire unit or the more elaborate three-bin unit opposite, you'll be adding a useful and valuable feature to your yard. A compost center will build fertile soil, producing healthy plants and vegetables—all the while putting yard and kitchen refuse back where it belongs. (Composting can even change your attitude toward lawn mowing. Some gardeners consider it harvesting compost, not cutting grass!)

GETTING READY

- For a long-lasting compost center, use redwood, cedar, or pressured-treated lumber, with galvanized or stainless-steel hardware.
- Choose a site close to your garden, but tucked away where appearances won't matter.
- Carefully position the corner posts, digging the holes deep enough to reach below the frost line.

MATERIALS LIST

- ☐ (4) 4"x4"x10' posts
- ☐ ½" galv. fencing, 4x20'
- ☐ (1) 1"x2"x8' bracing
- ☐ (4) 2"x4"x12' framing
- ☐ (2) ¾"x¾"x12' stop
- ☐ (2) 12' of 2x2 cleats
- ☐ (1) 1"x2"x18' top cleats
- ☐ (7) 1"x6"x12' slats
- ☐ (7) 2"x8"x12' decking
- ☐ (16) ⅜x3" lag bolts
- ☐ 6-ml plastic, 4x12'
- ☐ (24) ¾x3" brackets
- ☐ 1 pound each, 3" and 1½" deck screws

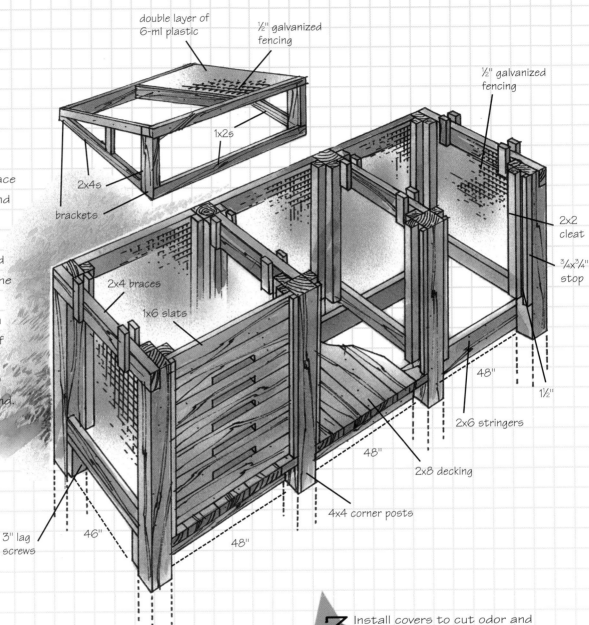

double layer of
6-ml plastic

½" galvanized
fencing

1x2s

2x4s

brackets

½" galvanized
fencing

2x2
cleat

¾x¾"
stop

2x4 braces

1x6 slats

48"

1½"

2x6 stringers

48"

2x8 decking

4x4 corner posts

3" lag
screws

46"

48"

1 Set the posts in place and attach front and back stringers using ⅜x3-inch lag screws. Level the stringers and plumb the posts. Fill the postholes with dirt or gravel, and tamp them firmly. Trim the tops of the posts so they are even, a minimum of 49 inches above the ground.

2 Notch the tops of the posts to "let in" the 2x4 horizontal bracing. (This bracing can be attached to the outside of the 4x4s if you wish to avoid notching the posts.) Attach the braces with 3-inch galvanized deck screws. Drill pilot holes and use 1½-inch deck screws to attach the ¾x¾-inch stops and 2x2 cleats to the front posts. Leave a ⅞-inch gap between them to allow for the 1x6 slats.

3 Install covers to cut odor and control moisture. Use ¾x3-inch brackets to fasten the joints. Add 1x2 cleats attached to the 2x4 braces to hold the covers in place. The covers simply slip in place from above, held between the 1x2s.

WATER SOURCES

If you have to haul out yards of garden hose every time the plants are thirsty, chances are they won't be watered as often as they should be. A water source handy to the garden makes regular watering easy. For a more permanent solution, consider adding an irrigation system. Here are two projects designed to get the moisture to where it is needed.

GETTING READY: REMOTE FAUCET

- If you plan to bury a water line, particularly in areas with cold climates, check with your local building department for recommended depths for water pipe. Also check with utility companies to be sure the projected lines won't interfere with other buried service lines.

- If you choose to run the supply line at ground level, plan a route that keeps it hidden along the base of a fence, or under bushes and shrubs.

MATERIALS LIST: REMOTE FAUCET

- ☐ (1) 4"x4"x5' post, (1) 2"x6"x12' for the border
- ☐ 16d galvanized nails
- ☐ ½" flexible PVC pipe
- ☐ bracket for hanging garden hose
- ☐ gate valve, galvanized T joint, 2 galvanized nipples
- ☐ 2 adapters for joining PVC to galvanized pipe
- ☐ self-draining faucet, 90° galvanized elbow, a length of galvanized pipe, and 2 pipe straps, Teflon tape

1 Shut off the water in your house and install a T-joint behind your outdoor faucet. Hook up the gate valve and nipples. Use Teflon tape for all connections.

2 Nail together a 3-foot-square border of 2x6s for the base of your remote faucet. Excavate a drainage area 6 inches deep. (If you are submerging your line, trench it to this spot.) Sink a 2-foot posthole and add 2 inches of gravel to the bottom of the hole. Set a 5-foot 4x4 in the hole.

3 Run the flexible line to the post. Connect a galvanized pipe to your supply line and fasten it to the post. Plumb the post, and pack the hole and the border area with gravel. Attach the faucet to the elbow. Use Teflon tape at the joints.

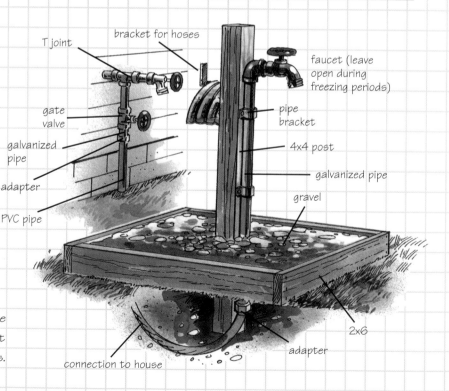

T joint

bracket for hoses

faucet (leave open during freezing periods)

gate valve

pipe bracket

galvanized pipe

4x4 post

adapter

galvanized pipe

PVC pipe

gravel

2x6

connection to house

adapter

GETTING READY:
DRIP IRRIGATION SYSTEM

- Plan your system, assigning drip emitters to permanent plants and soaker hose to row crops and annuals.
- Measure the length of your system and note the number of clamps, elbows, and T-joints needed.
- Climate and water quality often require varying components for these systems. Consult with your local plumbing supplier or garden center.

MATERIALS LIST:
DRIP IRRIGATION SYSTEM

- ☐ filter (for well water only)
- ☐ pressure regulator
- ☐ Wye connector
- ☐ solid drip tubing
- ☐ drip emitters
- ☐ soaker hose
- ☐ clamps

1 Connect the filter (if necessary) and pressure regulator to your water source. To supply more than one area, add a Wye connector to direct water to where it is most needed.

2 Perennial vegetable and fruit plants may warrant drip emitters. Be sure to select an emitter appropriate to the demands of the plants.

pressure regulator

filter

Wye connector

permanent or perennial plants

drip emitter

flexible pipe

annual row crops

hose clamps

soaker hose

3 Extend the system to the row crops by cutting the flexible pipe and adding T-connectors with clamps. Attach lengths of soaker hose to each T-connector.

4 Cover the soaker hose and emitters with straw mulch. This shields the moisture from evaporation until it can soak well into the ground.

DRAINAGE OPTIONS

Any yard must be ready to cope with exceptional accumulations of water, whether from sudden rainstorms or the slow melt of winter snows. Runoff from downspouts and expanses of concrete can create soggy areas that drown plants and infiltrate foundations. Long slopes, steep inclines, and low areas of lawn also can create problem areas. Any landscaping plan should anticipate and remedy these situations. Here are some options for improving the drainage of your lot.

GETTING READY

- You can accomplish a lot with a shovel and a wheelbarrow—if you take it slow. Otherwise, consider renting small earth-moving machines or hiring a landscaping contractor.
- If your project might affect another property—causing water to flow onto your neighbor's land, for example—consult with your local building department.
- Plan to incline drainage areas and drainpipes at a slope of ⅛ inch or more per foot of run.

trough pitched to direct water away

SWALE

A gentle trough, pitched to carry water away, can be dug into a slope to interrupt the flow of water. Plant a hardy ground cover in the trough.

ground cover

BAFFLE

A series of landscaping timbers set in a 2-inch gravel bed interrupts the flow of water on abruptly inclined slopes. Each timber should tilt toward the slope. For areas with serious runoff, position the timbers in zigzag fashion to slowly carry the water down the slope. The resulting mini-terraces are ideal for decorative planting.

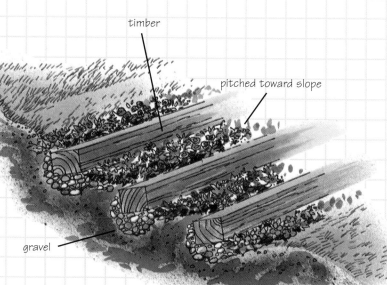

timber

pitched toward slope

gravel

CURTAIN DRAIN

Persistent underground water can be dealt with by digging a trench at least 2 feet deep (deeper as the drainpipe slope requires) and setting a perforated drainpipe in gravel. Above the gravel, a filter fabric keeps silt from clogging the system.

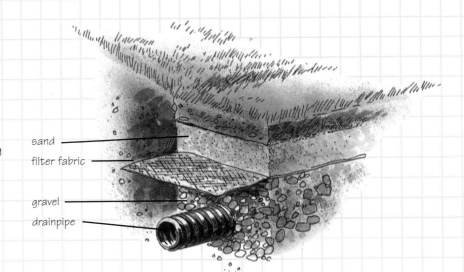

sand

filter fabric

gravel

drainpipe

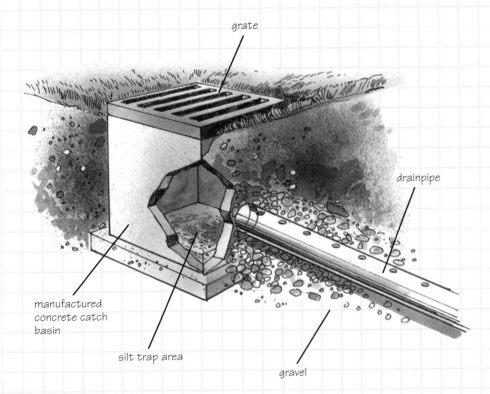

grate

CATCH BASIN

For areas where sudden and heavy rainfall frequently overloads normal drainage and soil absorption, a concrete catch basin can be installed to gather water. The drainpipe, pitched away from the catch basin, is connected high enough from the bottom of the basin to allow silt to accumulate in the trap. This project often requires professional planning and assistance.

drainpipe

manufactured concrete catch basin

silt trap area

gravel

281

INDEX

INDEX

THE USDA PLANT HARDINESS MAP
OF NORTH AMERICA

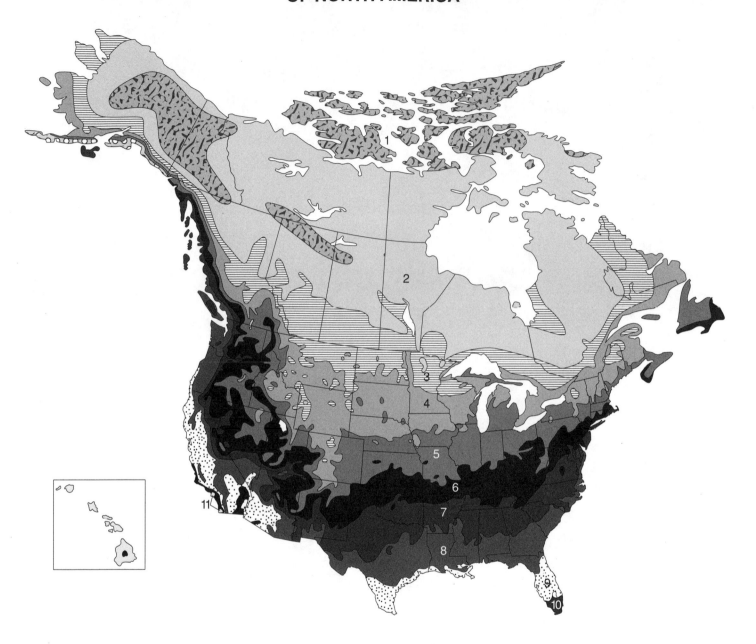

RANGE OF AVERAGE ANNUAL MINIMUM
TEMPERATURES FOR EACH ZONE

ZONE 1	BELOW -50° F	
ZONE 2	-50° TO -40°	
ZONE 3	-40° TO -30°	
ZONE 4	-30° TO -20°	
ZONE 5	-20° TO -10°	
ZONE 6	-10° TO 0°	
ZONE 7	0° TO 10°	
ZONE 8	10° TO 20°	
ZONE 9	20° TO 30°	
ZONE 10	30° TO 40°	
ZONE 11	ABOVE 40°	